The Dow Jones-Irwin Guide to Zero Coupon Investments

The Dow Jones-Irwin Guide to Zero Coupon Investments

DONALD R. NICHOLS

DOW JONES-IRWIN
Homewood, Illinois 60430

© DOW JONES-IRWIN, 1986

This publication is designed to provide accurate and
authoritative information in regard to the subject matter
covered. It is sold with the understanding that the
publisher is not engaged in rendering legal, accounting, or
other professional service. If legal advice or other expert
assistance is required, the services of a competent
professional person should be sought.

*From a Declaration of Principles jointly adopted by a Committee
of the American Bar Association and a Committee of Publishers.*

ISBN 0-87094-902-0
Library of Congress Catalog Card No. 86–71130

Printed in the United States of America

1 2 3 4 5 6 7 8 9 0 B 3 2 1 0 9 8 7 6

For My Wife Barbara

PREFACE

American investors have discovered zero coupon investments with a degree of enthusiasm that's surprised American financial markets. Since mid-1982, when several investment firms severed interest and principal certificates from Treasury securities and created a hybrid called a zero coupon bond, investors have purchased more than $100 billion of zero coupon investments.

Until recently, zeros were said to be useful only in IRAs and Keogh Plans because zero coupon investments, purchased at deep discounts to mature at a par of usually $1,000, normally generate a yearly tax liability even though they pay no yearly interest. IRAs and Keoghs permit tax-deferred growth, thereby avoiding taxation on zeros' "phantom interest." Now investors have discovered uses outside the IRA for an investment that offers profits, predictability, and a myriad of features.

In addition, the types of zero coupon investments have multiplied to include zero coupon certificates of deposit, original issue zeros from corporations, municipalities, and governments, zero coupon mutual funds and unit trusts, zero coupon commodity funds, and many others. There seems virtually no end to the varieties of zero coupon securities, and with innovations in products come innovative approaches to the uses of zeros in a total portfolio.

A balanced portfolio contains five elements: a savings component, a current income component, a capital growth component, an aggressive gains component, and a lump-sum accumulation component. Investors have discovered that zero coupon investments can serve all five of these critical portfolio elements. For example, U.S. Treasury bills and other zeros with short-term maturities provide capital stability and market-level returns that are ideal for savings.

Zero coupon CDs and intermediate-term zeros from corporations, municipalities, and other sources provide predictable
capital growth that often exceeds that of common stocks, the
conventional investment for capital growth. In addition, zeros
serve the growth component of the portfolio in many other
ways.

Convertible municipal bonds and EE Savings Bonds combine the features of long-term capital growth in securities that
become current income investments later in their lives. Further,
zero coupon investments can be serialized to provide current
income as they mature.

Long-term zero coupon bonds are highly volatile investments. Although their giant percentage fluctuations in price
discomfort conservative investors, aggressive investors can
profit from most zeros' intense sensitivity to interest rates
through active buying and selling.

The lump-sum component of the portfolio is designed to
accommodate anticipated needs for cash in the distant future—
for retirement, for example, or in accumulating funds for children's tuition. Yet the lump-sum component also has other
interpretations, for instance, in arranging steady payments
when converting retirement proceeds from an IRA Rollover or
distributions from an employee retirement plan. With their
predictable maturities, fixed interest rates, and known accumulations, many types of zero coupon investments are perfect for
the lump-sum component of the portfolio.

The only thing that seems greater than investors' appetite
for zeros is their appetite for information about them. To date,
much of that information has been sketchy, offered only in sales
literature from brokerages or from brief articles by financial
writers in personal finance magazines or newspaper investment
columns. There's been no single, comprehensive source of information about the total uses of zeros, and that's a situation this
book wants to correct.

The Dow Jones-Irwin Guide to Zero Coupon Investments will ac-
quaint you with the types of zero coupon investments and with
strategies you can use to manage them. There's no question that
zero coupon investments can literally accumulate to millions of
dollars, given sufficient time to grow. If you follow our orientation here, zeros can make you a great deal of money and serve
wise, reasoned uses in the total context of your life and portfolio.

The book is divided into three sections. Part One explains the different types of zero coupon investments, outlines their features pro and con, and deals with their facts and mechanics. Part Two of the book discusses strategies for assimilating zeros into coherent investment strategies. We'll place zeros in the context of the five portfolio elements and discuss their usefulness in specific types of accounts, such as the Uniform Gifts to Minors Account and the IRA. In addition, we'll see how zeros can help pattern portfolio planning around life events, such as mid-career crises, capitalizing a personal business, or arranging income for a time when your paycheck is less dependable. In the Appendix you'll find a glossary of common zero coupon terms, a reference for sources, brokers, and further information, and a worksheet for managing your portfolio of zeros.

As always, my orientation is the same as in my two previous Dow Jones-Irwin books, *Starting Small, Investing Smart* and *Life Cycle Investing:* Your understanding of an investment is necessary for you to make the most of it. In the case of zero coupon securities, the most is a great deal indeed.

DONALD R. NICHOLS

CONTENTS

Sum Component. Zero Coupon Securities and the Lump-Sum Component. Blending the Lump-Sum Component.

INTRODUCTION

Several years ago, Merrill Lynch, the major international brokerage firm and investment banker, hit upon an idea that made investors as much money as it made for brokers. Merrill Lynch purchased millions of dollars worth of U.S. Treasury bonds and reconfigured them into a new type of security that it called a Treasury Investment Growth Receipt—TIGR, for short. But this tiger had stripes of a different color.

In case you've never seen one, a conventional government bond is an ornate, green certificate about the size of typing paper. The bond is perforated into two sections: the first represents the U.S. Treasury Department's obligation to repay the principal—the amount you loaned the Treasury when you bought the bond—and the second section is subdivided into coupons representing your entitlement to semiannual interest payments—your return for lending the government money.

For example, let's say you bought a 20-year Treasury bond for $1,000 that paid interest of $50 every May and November. The first section of the bond declares the Treasury's obligation to pay you back your $1,000 (called par value) when the bond matures in 20 years, and the second half contains 40 small coupons that you could present to any bank in order to claim your $50 interest payments each May and November for 20 years.

Now imagine a stack of 100 bonds, each laid neatly atop the other. You know that in 20 years the Treasury will have to pay you $100,000 to redeem the par value of those 100 bonds ($1,000 × 100 bonds). What's more, every May and November the Treasury would have to pay you $5,000 ($50 × 100 bonds) when you presented the coupons.

That's an attractive vision, but it's cumbersome. Every six months you would have to clip all those coupons, and in 20 years you'd have to tote the bonds down to the bank to claim your repayment of principal. There's another problem: In order to receive the maximum return from your bonds, you'd have to reinvest each of those coupon payments in a savings account or money market fund. Because interest rates fluctuate, you wouldn't really know how much money you'd have from your total investment.

Merrill Lynch looked at its stack of bonds and noticed something interesting: The pile of coupons, all identical and all paying interest on the same day each May and November, resembled *one single bond.* The same was true of the halves of the bonds representing entitlement to principal. All of those were, in effect, like one bond when you put them all together. When it came down to cases, the government's $5,000 interest payment every May and November was no different from repaying $5,000 worth of principal every six months.

So Merrill Lynch asked, "Why not sell all of those coupons (and maybe the principal, too) as if they were one bond?"

The answer was, "Why not, indeed?"

However, there was one consideration. Investors demand interest as the price of lending money. Conventional government bonds (any bond, in fact) paid *coupon* interest to people who clipped the coupons every six months. If you resold all the coupons as one bond, how would you pay interest to lenders?

The answer: Sell the coupons and the principal as separate bonds but sell them at a price less than their terminal value.

Investors would then receive interest as the difference between what they paid and what the "bonds" were worth when they mature. That way Merrill Lynch wouldn't have to pay interim interest. Investors would make one investment, and at maturity they would receive one payment. For convenience, Merrill Lynch structured these reoffered TIGRs in par values of $1,000, the customary par of most bonds.

Out of this discovery came the "zero coupon bond" that paid "accreted" rather than coupon interest by "stripping" the coupon half of the bond from the par value half and selling them separately.

In the intricate mechanics of the thing, zero coupon bonds are a bit more complicated (escrow agents, transfer certificates, prospectuses, and the fact that government bonds more frequently exist on computer tape than in certificate form), but the concept functions with elegant simplicity: You buy the stripped security at one price, and when it matures you receive the newly created bond's par value, which is usually $1,000.

TIGRs became the cat's meow, if you'll pardon the pun, and they were followed by a bestiary of financial felines with similar names from other brokerages: CATS (Certificates of Accrual on Treasury Securities) from Salomon Bros. and LIONS (Lehman Investment Opportunity Notes) from Lehman Brothers. There are also COUGRS, ETRs, TBRs and the Treasury Department's book-entry zeros, called STRIPS (Separate Trading of Registered Interest and Principal of Securities). Whatever their species, they're all of the same genus.

These securities are "derivative zeros" because they're derived from an existing bond. However, many corporations and municipalities began floating "original issue zeros," which are originally issued as zero coupon bonds. No other security underpins them—only the issuer's obligation to pay par value upon maturity.

Banks and savings and loans caught the zero craze, and they began offering zero coupon certificates of deposit, which work just like zero coupon bonds except that they're CDs. More recently, mutual funds and municipal securities investment trusts have begun offering indirect investment in zero coupon bonds, much like standard stock and bond mutual funds.

Each form of zero coupon investment—and "investment" is more accurate than "bond" because now there are many types of zeros—offers an exceptional array of advantages.

- They provide highly predictable returns. If you hold a zero coupon security until maturity, you'll receive a stated par value—nearly always $1,000, although there are exceptions.
- They come in a range of maturities. You can buy a zero maturing tomorrow morning or one maturing in the next century.
- They escape "reinvestment risk"—the uncertainty associated with having to reinvest coupon payments at unpredictable rates.
- They can provide impressive returns, especially over longer maturities. For example, zero coupon CATS maturing in 2011 at a par of $1,000 can be purchased for

about $100. That's more than 10 times your money, and you can double, triple, or quadruple your capital with lesser maturities.

- As we'll see, some types of zeros offer special features that fit selected investment needs, making them even more attractive once you understand their singularities.
- Zero CDs and government bonds assembled by brokerages as zeros are virtually immune to default.

However, every investment has a catch, and zeros are no exception.

First, accreted interest from most zeros is usually taxable each year even though it's not paid until maturity. If you pay $500 for a zero coupon security maturing in 10 years at $1,000, the IRS usually expects to see some portion of the $500 accreted interest declared as current income every year. That's called taxation on phantom interest, and it's an issue we'll come back to.

Second, zeros are extremely volatile investments—that is, their prices fluctuate dramatically with moves in general interest rates. As we'll see, not all zeros are uniformly volatile, and for active traders the volatility of zeros is an attractive advantage.

Third, the prices for zeros, even for years of identical maturity, vary widely, so you have to shop carefully.

Finally, commissions are an important consideration to buyers of zeros, for reasons that we'll examine, and are somewhat higher as a percentage of initial investment than are commissions for other investments. There are, however, ways to minimize commissions, and after a little study you'll conclude that zeros are fully worth their commissions.

Zeros are incredibly popular for retirement-anticipation investments like IRAs, IRA Rollovers, and Keogh Plan Accounts because investors aren't taxed on zeros' phantom income in those accounts. Moreover, most zeros are specifically designed for IRAs, as they are often available in multiples of $2,000, the maximum yearly IRA contribution. Also, zeros are favored for Uniform Gifts to Minors Accounts because of their predictability and low cost and because phantom interest doesn't usually affect children's minimal tax brackets.

Yet many investors have seized upon zeros for their usefulness in other investment strategies. For example, U.S. Treasury bills and zeros with near-term maturities provide capital stability and liquidity plus market-level interest rates. They are excellent for the saver.

The most familiar zero is the EE Savings Bond, and it has features that make it compatible with other types of zero coupon investments. In fact, savings bonds offer some advantages that other zeros don't.

Many corporations have issued zero coupon bonds at attractive prices and yields. Broadly traded in public markets, corporate zeros provide ready liquidity and other advantages.

Municipal bonds issued as zeros pay federally tax-free interest and are appealing to high-bracket investors. They are so attractive that some investors prefer zero municipals over IRAs for retirement planning. What's more, innovations in the municipal bond market have created new and versatile municipal products, such as the convertible zero, which functions as both a zero coupon and conventional coupon bond and is a superb substitute for conventional annuities.

Astute brokerage houses have assembled packages of zero coupon bonds and retailed them in target funds, tax-exempt securities trusts, and zero coupon bond funds. Of great appeal to investors who prefer mutual funds or municipal investment trusts, indirect investment offers some exceptional opportunities over purchasing the zeros outright, including dollar cost averaging. In fact, one of the nation's most popular investment vehicles—the money market fund—is really a form of indirect investment in short-term zero coupon instruments like commercial paper, repurchase agreements, and Treasury bills.

New types of zeros are appearing almost daily in financial markets. For instance, there's a new investment program that mates zero coupon securities with commodities funds. Part of your investment goes into zeros and part is used for commodities speculation. Thanks to the predictability and security of zeros, you're guaranteed at least to break even, thereby removing downside risk while striving for upside potential from speculation in commodities.

Zero coupon certificates of deposit are available from banks or savings and loans and from brokerage firms that purchase conventional certificates of deposit and break them into small-denomination clusters. Because the underlying investment is issued by a depositary, zero CDs are insured by the FDIC or FSLIC, so they're excellent for investors who seek maximum security.

Finally, many investors aren't in the least distracted by non-municipal zeros' taxation on phantom interest. They actually *prefer* zeros over conventional securities *because* they pay no current income. These investors hold zeros happily along with conventional securities as a source of long-term capital accumulation.

Buy them for aggressive gains. Buy them for long-term growth. Buy them for tax-deferred or federally untaxed accumulations. Buy them for singular features. Buy them outright, or buy them in a professionally managed fund. Buy them for yourself, or buy them for your children.

With their versatility and diversity, zero coupon investments are excellent for many purposes and many types of investors and appropriate for many strategies. Whatever your preference or strategy, zero coupon securities can be important investments within your total portfolio. *The Dow Jones-Irwin Guide to Zero Coupon Investments* provides you the information you need to understand and manage zero coupon investments of all types.

We start by discussing the general nature of zeros—what they are, how they work, how to read their price quotations, how to calculate their approximate yields, and how to estimate tax on phantom interest. We cover each of the major types of zeros with attention to special features and uses. You'll learn the questions you need to ask when buying zeros and will familiarize yourself with the terms you'll encounter when your questions are answered. We'll also look at an extended section on managing a comprehensive portfolio of zero coupon investments throughout your life, give you a glossary of terms, and even provide a worksheet to use when managing your zeros.

Zero coupon securities are among the most popular and accessible of today's investments. With the information you're about to receive, they can also be the most profitable for you.

The Types of
Zero Coupon Investments

1

The Basics of
Zero Coupon Investments

As we examine zero coupon investments in more detail we'll become conversant with their many singular features. For now, however, we're concerned with understanding the basics of zeros, and those basics are price, yield, maturity, and par value. Price, yield, maturity, and par value are frustratingly related in the case of zeros, but it's not difficult to sort out the influences after you understand them.

The price of a zero coupon security is influenced by several considerations. The first is the quality of the issuer. "Quality" refers to the likelihood of the issuer's being able to pay off when the zero matures, which basically means that the quality of the zero equals the financial solvency of the issuer.

Price is also influenced by yield, just as yield is determined by price. Yield is your return for lending money. It's also the payment you receive to compensate for the risk of lending and for not consuming what you could have bought with the money you loaned. As a generality, the lower the price of a zero coupon investment, the higher is its yield (although, as we'll see, that's not always the case).

Yield is related to quality through the risk of default. That is, if you think someone has a very high likelihood of being able to repay your loan, you'll probably ask for less interest—a reduced yield—because his risk of default is (in your opinion, anyway) reduced.

Yield on zeros is determined by price, and both price and yield are functions of time. As a generality, the longer the maturity, the higher the yield because lenders assume greater risk in "lending long" and because they defer consumption for a longer period. Also, yield tends—but not always—to increase with time because investors usually must be induced to hold investments long term.

In the case of most zeros, however, prices and yields also are sensitive to the general level of interest rates in addition to the solvency of the issuer and the length of maturity. That's because zeros make only one payment of interest—at maturity—and must be held to maturity in order to receive that interest. Accordingly, the yield at which you purchased a zero is locked in for the life of the security, whereas general interest rates in the economy rise and fall. If interest rates rise, investors could be investing elsewhere for market-level returns, and they'll possibly sell their zeros to take advantage of higher yields in other investments. As we'll see, though, zeros' high "opportunity cost" can be an advantage.

Maturity also has an effect on prices and yields of zeros. Other considerations being equal, the longer the zero's length of maturity, the lower will be its price and, as a consequence, the higher will be its yield—up to a certain time. Also, the longer the term of maturity, the greater are the zero's opportunity cost and price fluctuations.

Nearly all zeros have a par value of $1,000, but there are some exceptions. Some zeros are indexed to other financial gauges like the inflation rate or rates on Treasury securities, so their par values may exceed $1,000 when they mature. These instruments will pay at least $1,000 upon maturity, however, except for EE Savings Bonds, which offer par values from $50 to $10,000 and are also indexed to the average interest rate on five-year Treasury securities. Their ultimate par values are difficult to determine, but we have parts of several chapters devoted to EE bonds. One type of zero, the U.S. Treasury bill, has a minimum par value of $10,000, and the minimum purchase is one bill. Zero coupon certificates of deposit have several par values, usually $1,000, $5,000, $10,000, and $100,000.

SURVEY OF RELATIONSHIPS

Let's take a look at the relationships we've established in isolation and then put them together.

First, quality is positively related to price. The higher the quality of the issuer, the higher will be the price of the zero compared to zeros of similar maturity from other issuers.

Second, quality is inversely related to yield. That follows, because price and yield are inversely related to each other. Higher prices mean lower yields. The higher the quality of the issuer, the lower will be the zero's yield.

Price is inversely related to time—the longer the maturity, the lower the price.

(Yield is *usually* positively related to time—the longer the maturity, the higher the yield. Having said so, however, we'll quickly learn that isn't always true.)

Like the rose, par value is par value, a buck's a buck, and $1,000 is $1,000—except in those few instances when par value is more than $1,000 because it's determined by minimum purchase requirements (like T-bills with $10,000 minimums) or by sliding interest calculations (as in zeros with yields geared to an index of some sort). These issues are special cases, and we'll discuss them fully later.

Before delving into the special cases, however, let's see how these considerations manifest themselves in public markets. First, let's take a look at a series of zero coupon bonds by the same issuer. We're not ready to learn how to read price quotations yet, and we're certainly not ready to learn how to calculate yields, so let's do this the easy way by having the price and yield quotations translated for us. The issues in question are Certificates of Accrual on Treasury Securities—the CATS featured in the Introduction. On any given day, you might see them quoted in *The Wall Street Journal* bond pages with these prices and maturities, just picking a few at random:

	Maturity Date	Price	Approximate Yield
CATS	1991	$555	10.50%
CATS	1992	510	10.25
CATS	1998	260	10.75
CATS	1999	231.25	11.00
CATS	2006–11	103.75	11.25–9.25

All of these issues are backed by U.S. government bonds, so quality of the issuer can't account for differences in prices and yields. We see most of the relationships confirmed. We see prices declining with time and yields increasing with time. There is, however, a perplexing aberration: the CATS of 2006–11. These zeros are unusual in several respects.

First, they feature two maturity dates—2006 and 2011. That's because these zeros are backed by Treasury bonds which are "callable" in 2006. In other words, during and after the year 2006, the government can call these bonds back from owners prior to terminal maturity in 2011. Consequently, the CATS derived from these bonds are also "callable." "Call features" are especially important with zero coupon municipal bonds, as we'll discuss in Chapter 4.

Second, although prices on these issues decline as maturity increases (the customary relationship), the yield increases only until 2006 and actually declines by 2011. That clearly isn't the customary relationship, for yields should increase with time. This aberration introduces two issues: yield to call and the effect of overall market relationships on zero coupon issues.

Whenever a zero is callable, investors must know the yield until the security is called because, as we see, yields can vary dramatically when call provisions are imposed. Again, this is a more important issue with zero coupon municipals than with other zeros. In this example, investors would prefer that the zero is called, for its yield to call is higher than its terminal yield, commonly called yield to maturity. That's not always the case, as we'll see.

The effect of overall market relationships is more serious and a more complicated issue. It's very difficult to say for certain why the yield to maturity falls for the CATS of 2006–11, but there are a couple possibilities.

For one, economies have a "term structure of interest rates" as a matter of course. In a highly inflationary economy, short-term rates (maturities under five years or so) may actually exceed long-term rates by several percentage points. That's because borrowers who issue securities would rather pay high rates for a short period than high rates for a long period. But even in more stable times, the structure of interest rates generally has a "yield elbow." Interest rates in general will increase over some term—say 20 years—and then decline modestly or sharply.

yield elbow = yield curve

If you were to draw a line through a chart of interest rates, the line would resemble a thin arm rising over some period and then declining. The point of decline is the elbow, and whether it bends sharply or gradually, early in the term structure of in- terest rates or late, depends on economic factors that are more mega-economic than macro-economic. It merely happens, and investors have to accept that it happens. Here is an illustration of the term structure of interest rates:

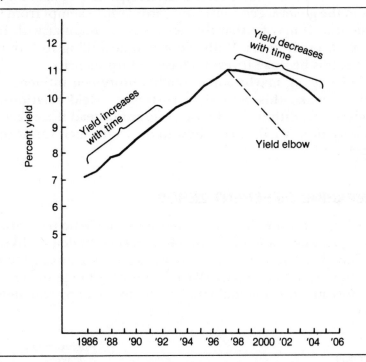

Sample illustration: term structure of interest rates

The horizontal axis represents time—in this hypothetical case, from six months to more than 20 years. The vertical axis represents yields available on U.S. Treasury securities. We've chosen Treasury securities because they're generally considered immune to default and, therefore, profitability considerations don't influence their prices and yields, as would be the case with corporate issues of identical maturity.

As you can see, yields increase out to a period of about 12 years, after which yields plateau and then dip a bit. The yield elbow occurs at about 12 years of maturity, indicating that the economy is offering its highest yields for 12-year maturities. Beyond maturities of 12 years, the economy does not offer commensurate yields to reward investing longer term.

But the term structure of interest rates isn't the only explanation of why yields on zeros—or any other investment—don't increase indefinitely. Another possible explanation of the declining yield to maturity of CATS 2006–11 is that securities markets have their own aberrations irrespective of the eccentricities in the general economy, and zeros aren't exempt from their influences. It may be that this zero is more popular with investors than other zeros. With more people willing to buy it, its yield is less because investors have bid up its price.

Then again, maybe some totally unforeseen influence is at work to make this zero defy customary yield relationships. Whatever: Question not the cause; grant instead the effect, and be aware of it. We'll discuss how to deal with such variations in Chapter 13.

COMPARING DIFFERENT ZEROS

Thus far, our example has covered only one issue of zeros, and that issue was available in public markets, tradeable like any publicly listed security. Many types of zeros petition for your attention, so let's compare. We'll examine a range of zero coupon investments and hold the maturity at approximately 10 years.

Investment	Price	Approximate Interest
$5,000 Zero Coupon CD	$2,508	7.35%
$5,000 EE Savings Bond	2,500	(see note 1 below)
$5,000 CATS of 1996	1,625	10.00
$5,000 Allied Corp. Zeros of 1996	1,600	10.60

Note 1: As we'll learn in the discussions of EE Savings Bonds, EEs pay a sliding rate of interest which increases the longer you hold the bond. EE bonds pay a minimum of 7.5 percent when held for their full 10-year maturity; held for at least five years, they pay 85 percent of the average interest rate for five-year Treasury notes. As of early 1986, EE bonds held five years were accreting at about 9.75 percent.

Note 2: Even though we're citing these zeros as 10-year issues, their prices and yields are being computed in late 1985. Consequently, as this is written these are closer to 11-year zeros. The table then is for instruction only.

In this case we've changed denominations to $5,000 just to vary our examples a bit. Each of these investments has approximately the same maturity, varying only by a few months (for example, the Allied-Signal Corp. issue matures in late December 1996, whereas the CATS mature in mid-May 1996), yet prices and yields differ markedly, as do other circumstances pertaining to each zero. These price and yield quotations are very approximate, changing daily, yet they illustrate some of the trade-offs that investors make when buying zero coupon securities.

Note that the zero CD and the EE Savings Bonds have the highest prices and lowest yields. However, the former, being issued by an institution backed by the Federal Savings and Loan Insurance Corporation, and the latter, being an obligation of the U.S. government, are highly secure against default, and neither fluctuates in price as do the other zeros in our example. Further, the accreted interest on the zero CD is fully taxable, whereas the interest on the EE bond is exempt from state tax.

As you'd expect, the yield on the CATS is slightly lower than the yield on the corporate zero of the same maturity. That the CATS are derived from U.S. government securities probably explains the differential—better security against default. Bear in mind, however, that both issues will fluctuate in price (unlike the first two) and that commissions aren't charged to purchase zero CDs and EE Savings Bonds.

Why would an investor prefer a lower-yielding zero over a higher-yielding one? Much of the rest of the book is devoted to answering this question, but we can introduce now some considerations that we'll cover at length later.

PREFERENCES AND STRATEGIES FOR ZEROS

We've already surmised that some investors are willing to accept a lower yield because of the safety, stability and absence of commissions associated with zero CDs and savings bonds. Such investors resent the commissions and resist the capital fluctuations of publicly traded zeros, nor would they go near some of the other types of zero coupon investments that we'll study.

Investors who buy zeros intending to hold them to maturity aren't concerned with interim capital fluctuations. All they care about is that their zeros mature to par value. Accordingly, you'd expect investors following the buy-and-hold strategy to prefer the highest yielding zero, which is the Allied-Signal Corp. zero in our example. For some investors, that would be the preferred investment because its yield is highest. However, other investors would prefer the CATS because of their claim against Treasury bonds. These buy-and-hold investors are willing to sacrifice a bit of yield for added security.

For another thing, the ease of purchasing EE bonds and zero CDs, or other types of zeros, may offset their reduced yield for some investors. Some investors find the convenience of buying zeros where they bank or where they have their brokerage accounts to be worth a little yield. (By the way, the same can be said of buying other types of zeros, for example, buying savings bonds where you work, buying convertible municipals from your municipal bond broker, or buying shares in a zero bond fund from a mutual fund family in which you already invest.)

Some investors aren't interested in the yield on zeros at all because they don't intend to hold them until maturity. They intend to play zeros for capital appreciation—an aggressive strategy that we'll look at—and to do so they must buy zeros traded in open markets or in markets maintained by brokers from whom they bought their zeros.

The zeros of Allied-Signal Corp. and the CATS are listed on public exchanges. Like all listed securities, including many other issues of zeros, markets are maintained by middlemen, and prices are established by the public's demand for the securities as well as by the conditions we outlined at the start of this chapter. These zeros can be bought and sold any time because the public market maintains liquidity. Therefore, they're favored by aggressive investors because their mechanics make it possible to buy and sell them.

But some conditions might impair the liquidity (ability to buy and sell) of other types of zeros. Those conditions dissuade aggressive investors, but they're also important for others who invest in zeros to be aware of.

For example, EE Savings Bonds can't be redeemed before you've owned them six months. That's the law, and there are no exceptions, but after six months you can sell them anywhere at a price established by the government, not the market. Despite the many advantages of EE Savings Bonds, which we'll study in later chapters, they are absolutely illiquid for six months and their prices are determined by fiat, not financial markets.

Neither condition bothers some investors and investment strategies; both are intolerable for others.

Next, some zeros don't have public or private markets. For example, if you buy a zero coupon certificate of deposit from a bank or savings and loan, it may have the same constraints that impair the liquidity of other CDs. A certificate of deposit is a contractual obligation. You agree to leave funds on deposit for a specific period, at the end of which the institution agrees to pay a specified face value. Under some conditions, if you redeem a zero CD before it matures, you will be subject to interest penalties. In effect, the zero CD generally isn't liquid, although some large-denomination zero CDs and zero CDs purchased through brokerages are. Lack of liquidity doesn't bother investors following a buy-and-hold strategy, but it can trouble other investors greatly.

Another condition influencing liquidity pertains to zeros purchased from sponsoring brokerages. For each issue of a corporate or derivative zero that enters public markets, scores of other issues are purchased privately by financial institutions that sell them to customers. Most major brokerage firms maintain inventories of their own zeros or zeros from other institutions, including zero CDs plus corporate and derivative zeros. They frequently will maintain a market in these issues. When you buy or sell zeros, your broker will execute transactions from the firm's inventory at prices the brokerage and the market establish. This can be advantageous, because you won't pay commissions on these trades, unlike zeros traded through public markets. However, the brokerage isn't obligated to "make a market," and under some conditions it may be reluctant to do so. The prospect is remote but possible, and you should be aware of the possibility when you buy zeros directly from a sponsoring brokerage.

With large denomination CDs—face values of $100,000 or more—the selling brokerage firm or depositary might make a market in the zero. In other words, unlike conventional zero CDs suited only for the buy-and-hold strategy, large denomination zero CDs are sometimes liquid. You can buy and sell these zero CDs, subject to the same warning about zero bonds purchased from a sponsoring brokerage. If there's any chance you'll not hold any zero until maturity, buy it from an institution that intends to make a market or from public markets.

READING PRICE QUOTATIONS

It's time that we learned to read zero coupon bond quotations from the financial pages. If you buy zeros from some sources, you'll receive a conventional dollar price quotation and yield: The investment literature will read something like "$1,759 for a yield of 10.10 percent." But most of the time zeros are quoted in financial code. Here's a quotation for a corporate zero from *The Wall Street Journal*, although derivative zeros and municipal zeros are similarly quoted.

Issuer	Volume	High	Low	Close	
AlldC zr96	17	32¼	32	32	− ¼

The issuer is Allied-Signal Corporation. If you're perplexed about the identity of an issuer, check with a broker or consult a stock market quotation guide. The "zr" identifies the issue as a zero, and "96" is the maturity date of 1996. The "17" is trading volume—17 bonds or $17,000 in par value changed hands—followed by the high-low-close prices and comparison with the previous day's close, off fractionally here.

To read price quotations, convert fractions to decimals. In this case, 32¼ becomes 32.25. Multiply by 10, giving 322.50. Add a dollar sign, and you're done. The opening price of this zero on the New York Bond Exchange was $322.50. The low price during the day's trading was $320, and the closing price was $320. At that price, the bond was selling for $2.50 less than the previous day (that is, ¼ = .25 × 10 = $2.50).

Zero coupon municipal bonds are also quoted in dollars per hundred, which means you must multiply quotations by 10 to convert prices to $1,000 par value. In most instances, though, municipal zeros aren't quoted in fractions. For example:

Sam Rayburn Tx Mun Pwr Agy Pwr Sup Sys Rv 9/1/12 at 7.379

In this case, the issue is a revenue bond floated by the municipal power agency in Sam Rayburn, Texas, maturing in September 2012. We'll learn more about municipal zeros in Chapter 4. The item of interest is the price: 7.379.

To decipher the figure, multiply by 10, giving 73.79. Add a dollar sign, and we've figured out that the zero can be bought for $73.79 per $1,000 par value.

A THUMBNAIL GUIDE TO CALCULATING YIELDS

For the most part, buying zeros presents no complicated mathematical problem. Purchase price is quoted by a dealer or in the financial pages. Your zeros will be worth $1,000 when they mature, for $1,000 is the customary par value of zeros. And usually you know the implied interest rate because your broker or sales literature quoted it to you.

Unfortunately, though, maybe you'll see a zero in the bond pages while your broker isn't available to figure the yield, or perhaps you'll want to confirm a quoted interest rate with your own calculations. Such occasions require you to calculate yield on a zero coupon security—the approximate yield, that is, because the accurate yield changes from minute to minute. Fortunately, most of us don't need to know the yield of a zero to the ultimate decimal, and all we need for a serviceable calculation is a compound interest table.

If you're not familiar with the concept of compound interest, the basic idea is that $1 to be received today is worth $1, whereas someone's promise to give you $1 tomorrow ought to "be worth" less than $1 to accommodate risk of lending, forsaken consumption, and a return for investing. A zero coupon security promises to pay $1,000 tomorrow for an investment today, so you'd expect it to sell for less than $1,000. How much less depends upon the circumstances we noted early on. The price for and yield of money received in the future is a "present value computation," and you calculate the present value with the table labeled "Present Value of $1" from a compound interest table.

Some form of compound interest table is found in nearly every college finance book. For the novice, a useful text is *Compound Interest and Annuity Tables* by Jack C. Estes (New York: McGraw-Hill, 1976). Advanced students of interest and time value of money should read *The Dow Jones-Irwin Guide to Interest* by Lawrence R. Rosen (Homewood, Ill.: Dow Jones-Irwin, 1981). In addition, modestly sophisticated pocket calculators have compound interest features that enable you to calculate yield without knowing what you're calculating.

In this case what we're doing is estimating the interest rate—or yield. Price, maturity, and par value are known, but the interest yield created by the difference between price and par is unknown. Let's take the example of the Allied-Signal Corp. zero maturing in 1996, quoted at a price of $320 for maturity in approximately 11 years as of late 1985.

In establishing a price of $320, the market tells us that $1,000 to be received in 11 years from this issuer is worth $320 today. In other words, the present value of $1,000 is $320. Our question is, "$1,000 is worth $320 today according to what rate of interest?" We turn to a present value table in our book of compound interest tables, and through trial and error, under columns of figures for 11-year maturities, we find these entries:

Years	10% Nominal Annual Rate	10.5% Nominal Annual Rate	11% Nominal Annual Rate	11.5% Nominal Annual Rate
11	0.3418	0.3244	0.3079	0.2923

These numbers declare the present value of $1 to be received 11 years from now. To find the present value of $1,000, multiply by 1,000. Accordingly, at a 10.5 percent nominal rate of interest, $1,000 to be received 11 years from now is worth $324.40. At 11 percent nominal interest, $1,000 to be received 11 years from now is worth $307.90.

The price of $320 falls between the $324.40 that indicates a 10.5 percent yield and the $307.90 representing an 11 percent yield. Reasoning with given information about price and years to maturity, we see that today's price of $320 represents a yield between 10.5 and 11 percent and much closer to 10.5 percent than 11 percent.

This figure is the approximate yield to maturity of the zero—the yield you'd receive if you held the zero for its full term of maturity. To find yield to call, substitute the call date for the maturity date.

We've used the present value schedule for semiannual compounding. Even though zeros are presumed to pay phantom annual interest, their yields and sometimes tax consequences are calculated using semiannual compounding tables, as they would be for coupon-paying bonds.

Rather than go through such torturous examination of present value tables, most of us will wait until our broker is free or trust the bank's quoted yield. That can be a mistake. On several occasions your author has noted serious discrepancies between stated and actual yields in investment literature, particularly in literature from banks and S&Ls quoting prices and yields on zero coupon certificates of deposit.

TAX CONSEQUENCES OF
ZERO COUPON INVESTMENTS

It's important to know the yield on your zeros because that's the basis upon which you must calculate annual tax liability. As we've noted, zeros usually produce phantom taxable income yearly even though they don't produce any actual interest until maturity. However, not all zero coupon investments are taxed the same. Taxation on zeros held outside IRAs and Keoghs is *exceedingly* complicated—more complicated than we could possibly cover, even though we'll attempt to do so now and throughout the book.

Before we proceed further on this subject, know this: If you're going to buy any zero coupon investment, you must request copies of IRS Publication 1212 ("List of Original Issue Discount Obligations") and IRS Publication 550 ("Investment Income and Expenses"). Both are free for the asking from the IRS. The former publication discusses how to compute tax liability on zero coupon investments of many types and provides an exhaustive (but by no means definitive) list of corporate and derivative zeros and computed yearly interest liability per $1,000 par value. It is absolutely indispensable if you're going to invest in zeros, and you must be sure to request an updated issue from the IRS each year. Publication 550 is a useful cross-reference.

In computing your yearly tax liability from zeros held outside tax-deferred accounts, there are a thousand qualifications. Your situation will have to be examined on a case-by-case basis depending on whether you bought the zero when it was originally issued or in a secondary market, when the zero was issued regardless of when you purchased it, whether you inherited it, and the type of zero. Within these ranges, you pay phantom interest tax either yearly or when you dispose of the bond. You will calculate that interest on a straight-line constant interest method, or you will use a compound interest calculation as if the zero were a conventional coupon-paying bond.

The following is only an illustration and a guide to understanding the complexity of the problem in assessing tax liability on zeros held outside IRAs and Keoghs. Moreover, changes in tax laws might reverse any of these circumstances. You must keep current by continuing to study IRS publications and rulings, and as more zero coupon products are introduced more tax changes will appear. The following discussion is a useful basic guide in assessing the tax status of zeros.

Corporate Zeros Issued before May 28, 1969, and Government Obligations Issued before July 2, 1982

The investor pays no tax on accreted interest until the year in which the obligation is sold, exchanged, or redeemed. If you sell the zero at a loss, the entire loss is a capital loss and no reporting of accreted interest is required. If you sell the zero at a capital gain, a portion of the return will be taxed as interest income and the remainder will be taxed at capital gains rates.

To determine interest liability for zeros issued during this period, you execute three calculations:

1. Divide the number of full months you owned the obligation by the number of full months from date of issue to date of maturity.
2. Subtract your purchase price from $1,000.
3. Multiply the two numbers.

That calculation tells you how much interest is taxed. If your selling price is greater than accreted taxation, the amount by which it is different is a capital gain. If your selling price is less than what you should have received after calculating accreted interest, the entire loss is a capital loss, and you owe no tax on interest.

Corporate Obligations Issued after May 27, 1969, but before July 2, 1982

A. If you bought these zeros *when they were originally issued,* you're in luck because the issuing corporation is obligated to supply you a completed IRS Form 1099-OID showing the amount of accreted interest you owe for that tax year. For zeros issued during this period, you're expected to declare phantom interest income each year, but the issuer has to tell you how much.

However, the calculations are performed for you only if you held these zeros for the entire year. If you owned these zeros for part of a year, you have to figure your taxable phantom interest yourself:

1. Subtract purchase price from par value to determine the original issue discount.
2. Divide the original issue discount by 12.
3. Multiply the result by the number of full and partial months you owned the zero.

That figure is taxable phantom interest.

B. If you bought zeros issued during this period after they were originally issued—that is, if you bought them in secondary markets—you still receive IRS Form 1099-OID, but it's probably useless. Fortunately, IRS Publication 1212 will probably reveal the amount of phantom interest you need to declare in this situation.

All Zeros Issued after July 1, 1982, and before January 1, 1985

A. If you bought these zeros *when originally issued* and held them for the entire year or that part of the year after original issue, you'll again receive Form 1099-OID telling you how much phantom interest to declare.

B. If you bought these zeros *when originally issued* but did not hold them for the full year, divide the original issue discount by 366 and multiply the result by the number of days (days, not months as in the previous case) you held the zeros.

C. If you bought these zeros *after original issue,* you'll again receive Form 1099-OID, and again it will probably be useless. If the zero is listed in IRS Publication 1212, you're in luck, because the publication will reveal the amount of taxable phantom interest per bond. If the zero isn't listed in the publication, you will have to calculate phantom taxable interest yourself. To do that you follow these steps:

1. Contact the issuer of the zero to discover the original issuing price and original yield to maturity.
2. Multiply the two numbers and divide by 366.

3. Multiply the resulting figure by the number of days you held the zeros.

This procedure is called "constant interest corresponding to the accrual period." It's used only for zeros issued between July 1, 1982, and January 1, 1985.

All Zeros Issued after December 31, 1984

Phantom taxable interest on these zeros is taxable yearly according to the semiannual compound interest formula used on conventional bonds:

1. Multiply the zeros' yield to maturity times the cost of the zeros.
2. Multiply that figure times one half.

The result is the amount of taxable phantom interest for the first half year you owned the zeros.

To determine phantom taxable interest for the second half year, add the result of the calculation above to the purchase price of the bond and repeat steps one and two above. This gives you the total phantom taxable interest for one full year of ownership for bonds issued after December 31, 1984.

Each six months that you owned the bond forms the basis upon which you compute phantom taxable interest for the next six-month period. For example, say that you paid $10,000 for an issue of zeros yielding 10.5 percent. To determine phantom taxable interest for a six-month period:

$$\$10,000 \times 10.5\% \times .5 = \$525$$

For the second six-month period, add $525 to the purchase price and recalculate:

$$\$10,525 \times 10.5\% \times .5 = \$552.56$$

For a full year of phantom taxable interest, add the two sums:

$$\$525 + \$552.56 = \$1,077.56$$

When figuring phantom taxable interest for the next six-month period, your basis for calculation becomes $11,077.56 ($10,000 + 1,077.56).

The preceding has been a quick recitation of how to compute taxable phantom interest on publicly traded zero coupon securities issued during the specified times. You shouldn't rely upon it as a guide in computing your taxes, however. By all means, consult the referenced IRS publications when you're completing Form 1040 and Schedule B for interest declarations.

In computing phantom interest taxation on other types of zero coupon investments, such as zero coupon CDs, zero coupon bond funds, and T-bills, you'll be assisted by paperwork from the issuing authority. We'll cover the tax consequences in the chapters pertaining to those types of zeros.

For now, you need to be aware that zeros do generate tax on phantom interest income when you hold them outside tax-deferred accounts. Whether that tax is declarable yearly or upon maturity or disposition of the zeros depends upon when they were issued. Because the tax computations are so complicated, many investors restrict their holdings of corporate and derivative zeros to IRAs and Keoghs, which don't require declaration of phantom income until you begin taking receipts from your account upon retirement or permanent disability. However, if you're willing to do a little paperwork, you can triumph over the tax complexities of zeros and use them effectively outside IRAs and Keoghs.

SUMMARY

We've looked at the basics of what zeros are, how they work, what determines their prices and yields, and why investors might prefer one over the other. But there are many more types of zero coupon investments with many more strategies and advantages. We need to examine the different types of zeros so that we can learn how the advantages of each can be applied to a total portfolio.

2

Derivative Zero Coupon Bonds

Derivative zeros—also called reoffered zeros—are so named because they are derived from other types of bonds. As we saw in the Introduction, CATS and TIGRs and other financial felines are created from conventional Treasury bonds by stripping interest and principal portions of the bond certificate and selling each separately. The new instrument created is derived from a previous bond and reoffered to buyers in its new form.

These are not original issue zeros, which we'll cover in the next chapter, because they are not, straightforwardly enough, originally issued as zero coupon securities as are other types of corporate, government or municipal obligations. For the most part, their status as second generation bonds is a matter of more curiosity to students of financial terms than to investors, but there is one term we have to raise, and that term is *government-backed.*

Read any advertisement for CATS or TIGRs or any of the other financial felines created by brokerage institutions, and you'll see they're billed as "government-backed securities." That claim isn't false, but it is both true and not true. It's true in that the securities from which these zeros are derived are backed by the full faith and credit of the U.S. government. It's not true in that the U.S. government and the Department of the Treasury do not back *the zeros themselves* directly with their full faith and credit or taxing power.

When Merrill Lynch, Salomon Bros. or E.F. Hutton creates

26

derivative zeros, it purchases the Treasury bonds from which the zeros are created directly. The Treasury bonds are backed by the full faith and credit of the U.S. government. The brokerage is the owner of record, and the brokerage has the claim upon the Treasury's backing, not the investor who bought the derivative zeros. The brokerage then places the Treasury bonds in permanent escrow with a major bank. Those escrowed bonds are then stripped of principal and interest and reoffered as zeros. The escrowed bonds are in reality the backing for the zeros, not the Treasury. The Treasury backs the bonds from which the zeros are created, but the Treasury doesn't back the zeros themselves.

However, this is not to say that the advertisers are being misleading. In this context, "government-backed" is merely financial shorthand. The only way these bonds will default is if the Treasury repudiates its debt, if the escrow agent does something dishonest with the escrowed securities, and if the brokerage refuses to make payment when the zeros are due. None of these is likely to happen singly, and fundamentally all three parties would have to renege simultaneously before the LIONS or TIGRs or CATS would be out of the bag that you're left holding. So we can use the term *government-backed* honestly although somewhat imprecisely, and we'll refer to derivative zeros as government-backed just as brokerages do in their advertising.

We can think of CATS and TIGRs and other financial felines as close proxies for Treasury bonds and regard them with all the security due a Treasury obligation. As of early 1986, no one has stripped corporate bonds and reoffered them as zeros (although corporations have issued their own zeros), so the term *derivative zeros* refers only to zeros created from Treasury bonds. As we'll see in the next chapter, some zeros—like EE Savings Bonds and T-bills—are backed directly by the Treasury or by government organizations like the Government National Mortgage Association that are presumed to have the government's full faith and credit behind them.

CHARACTERISTICS OF DERIVATIVE ZEROS

Like all of the zeros we'll examine, derivatives have four important characteristics: price, interest rate, maturity, and par value. As we saw in Chapter 1, these four characteristics are interrelated.

Price is straightforward enough. You pay what you pay whether you're buying zeros in public markets or through a broker's inventory. You learned how to translate price quotations in Chapter 1, so now you can perform that all important step: shopping around for the best prices. Remember, it's not at all uncommon to find derivatives of similar or identical maturity selling at considerable differences in price.

We've also looked at interest rates and what they mean not only for accumulations but also for tax on phantom interest. We know that all zeros pay interest as the difference between purchase price and par value, and that the accretion in price to par is measured as accreted interest.

Derivative zeros come in virtually as many maturities as do government bonds, which shouldn't be surprising considering where derivatives come from.

Par value is an easy concept when you're talking about derivative zeros. It's $1,000 for all of them. No one has yet created derivatives with sliding interest payments resulting in par of more than $1,000.

ADVANTAGES OF DERIVATIVE ZEROS

The chief advantage of derivative zeros is their high security against default. Many investors like to hold derivatives in Individual Retirement Accounts, and some investors like to purchase long-term zeros to maximize capital accumulations. They can buy long-term derivatives with confidence, knowing there's an exceedingly slim likelihood of default.

Additionally, brokerages often strip Treasury bonds for the specific purpose of making them attractive for IRAs and Keoghs. At present the maximum IRA investment is $2,000 per individual investor. Brokerages often structure prices so that you can purchase derivatives in even increments of $2,000. This makes the mathematics simple in more ways than one, as each derivative you buy will mature to $1,000. Let's say that a particular feline is priced at $200. Not only do you know you can buy 10 of them, but you also know you will have $10,000 when they mature.

Derivative zeros' close proximity to Treasury bonds makes them attractive to aggressive investors who want short-term price appreciation from fluctuations in interest rates. Highly secure against default, derivatives don't have default risk built.

into their prices; prices are determined almost exclusively by the term structure of interest rates. As we'll see in Part Two when we discuss zeros' uses in each of the five portfolio components, aggressive investors prefer derivatives for quick gains because they are straightforward interest rate plays.

Derivatives' broad selection of maturities serves investors of many orientations, not merely those who want long-term zeros in a buy-and-hold IRA strategy or those who expect to trade them frequently for price appreciation. Short-term and inter-mediate-term maturities, those of less than 5 years and from 5 to 10 years, are useful in many portfolio strategies. We'll cover them in Part Two in separate chapters devoted to zero coupon investments and each of the portfolio elements.

DISADVANTAGES OF DERIVATIVE ZEROS

The disadvantages of derivatives are the same as for almost any zero coupon security, and the first is their intense volatility. Felines are exceedingly sensitive to changes in interest rates— more so than other bonds. Price volatility is ideal for aggressive investors who can take advantage of price fluctuations, but it's unnerving for most investors. Derivatives with near-term ma-turities are less sensitive to price fluctuations, but even they act more erratically than conventional bonds of similar maturity. Therefore, if you're going to invest in derivatives, you have to tolerate capital fluctuations.

Second, as we've already mentioned, prices for derivatives of similar or identical maturity can vary widely among sponsors and markets. Even though all derivatives are virtually the same product, price differences can be 25 percent or more. This fact makes shopping for the best prices a more difficult and time-consuming proposition.

Third, commissions can be a formidable charge when you're buying derivatives, and commissions (or their equivalent) aren't uniform. Commissions are important to buyers of zeros because they're fairly high as a percentage of investment, because zeros don't pay interim interest to offset commissions, and because commissions can reduce yield to maturity.

Probably the least expensive way to buy zeros is directly from the inventory of the sponsoring brokerage. When you buy CATS on the open market from a full-service broker, you'll pay a straight commission (at present, other felines aren't sold through listed exchanges, although Merrill Lynch has shown some intention to list its TIGRs). If you buy them from the sponsor, you'll be charged a basis price. Basis pricing is the equivalent of a commission, but it's usually less. Also, you can buy zeros from some discount brokerages—those that offer only order execution—for a flat fee plus a small charge per bond.

The most frequently cited "disadvantage" of zeros is their failure to pay current income while they generate a current tax liability from phantom interest. Of course, many recommended investments like raw land, precious metals, collectibles, and many growth stocks pay no current income, yet they often involve taxes, carrying charges, insurance fees, safe deposit rentals, appraisal costs, and other detractions.

In addition, many investors don't regard phantom interest taxation as particularly burdensome. We'll mention this point in other contexts, but it's important that we mention it here because many investors think derivatives are appropriate only for tax-deferred accounts.

First, let's be honest about what really happens with investment income. Too often, we spend it instead of reinvesting it, and we wind up with little more than we started with. We also pay taxes on that dissipated income. Even if you have to pay taxes on phantom interest yearly, at least you'll have capital accumulations when your zeros mature. That's better than looking back on all the coupon interest payments you squandered while you're totaling up your yearly interest payments.

Second, investors are accustomed to paying taxes on interest income that's reinvested, and, in effect, your phantom interest payments are reinvested for compounded growth as zeros approach maturity. Thus, the tax situation on zeros is no more onerous than customary for reinvested income.

Third, proposed revisions to the tax code promise to remove tax-deferral features of other types of investments. Already, the discounts on conventional bonds issued after mid-1984 are taxable yearly along with their coupon payments. Many economists and politicians have proposed to tax the hitherto untaxed accumulations in annuities and the capital growth in other types of insurance products. If enacted, these proposals are but a step from taxation on the unreceived appreciation in stocks, homes, rental property, real estate, and other investments that have appreciated in value while you own them. If these investments become taxable as current income, zeros will be no more disadvantaged than these vehicles, and they'll have predictable accumulations besides, which no other investment offers.

The bottom line about taxation on phantom interest is that this circumstance isn't as awful as it's made out to be. What's more, if you're in minimal tax brackets and are building a portfolio, it may make sense for you to pay taxes as you go, for when your zeros mature you'll have created a pool of capital for reinvestment.

SUMMARY

Until someone decides to pull a neat trick with corporate bonds, derivative zeros are defined as reoffered investments created by stripping Treasury bonds from their interest and principal coupons. These vehicles are highly safe, liquid, and convenient. They're useful in a variety of investment strategies, as we'll see in Part Two, and they don't have to be held in tax-deferred accounts to receive their full potential as investments.

So long as you're aware of the price differences and variance in commissions among similar zeros from different sources, you can avoid some of the disadvantages associated with this singular new investment vehicle. And so long as you're not blind to deficiencies in conventional wisdom, you needn't fear to take advantage of zeros outside tax-deferred accounts.

Derivatives are merely the first of scores of differing types of zero coupon investments. We have many more to cover, so let's move on to the next chapter, which discusses bonds originally issued as zeros and not created as zeros out of another investment.

3

Original Issue
Zero Coupon Investments

To be rigorous in use of financial terms, any investment that's issued with an original discount—that is, with a price less than its par value—is a zero coupon security. Well-capitalized investors and financial institutions have been dealing in several types of zeros for many years. Some types of commercial paper (short-term obligations of corporations), repurchase agreements (sell-and-buy-back arrangements with government bonds), and even commercial letters of credit (issued by one financial institution and salable at a discount to another) could legitimately qualify as zero coupon securities.

For most private investors, however, the initial purchase price of these instruments is beyond reach, for they're customarily denominated in the millions of dollars. Nonetheless, there are several types of original issue zeros that are well within the reach of private investors, and you may own some of them without having ever thought of them as zeros. What separates original issue zeros from derivative zeros like CATS and TIGRs is that they're originally offered to investors at discounts from par. They aren't derived from any other investment.

Some original issue zeros—zero coupon municipal bonds, for example—have attained broad public markets and are so useful to private investors that we've devoted the next chapter to them. Others have billions of dollars in par value outstanding, and we're about to take a look at them. Original issue zeros are exactly like derivative zeros in their particulars, except, of course, that they're backed only by the issuer's promise to pay par value upon maturity and aren't underpinned by another type of bond.

First, let's look at zero coupon investments issued directly by the U.S. Treasury. These are direct obligations of the U.S. government and are backed by the full faith and credit of Uncle Sam.

EE SAVINGS BONDS

At bottom, today's zero coupon bonds, including some of the more sophisticated alternatives we'll examine in later chapters, are little more than extensions of the original zero coupon bond—the Series E (now Series EE) Savings Bond. What's more, the original zero coupon bond is still the easiest, most accessible, and most convenient of all the zeros available today.

Even though EE bonds are the grandfather of all zeros, they have several singular features that make them different from later generations. Or, to be more accurate, EE Savings Bonds contain nearly all the features that contemporary zeros have inherited singly, as we'll see in later chapters. Thus, EE bonds are the least like any single issue of zeros, but they're the most like all of them examined together. That's frequently the way it is with the senior ancestor of any family.

Consequently, we have to start with EE bonds. By understanding them and their uses you can understand the zeros that followed them, and, in understanding the usefulness of other zeros, you will understand EE bonds.

The familiar EE bond works like the zeros that we discussed in the Introduction. It's sold at discount from par value and pays accreted interest as the difference between purchase price and par value of the bond. However, there are several major differences between EE bonds and other zeros.

First, par values of EE bonds are $50, $75, $100, $200, $500, $1,000, $5,000, and $10,000, whereas par for other zeros is nearly always $1,000.

Second, you buy all EEs at half of par value. A $50 EE bond costs $25. A $10,000 EE bond costs $5,000. With other zeros, you pay a price that decreases with the lengthening maturity of the bond.

Third, the maturity of all EE bonds is 10 years (with the exception of a feature called extended maturity, which we'll mention in Chapter 12). Other zeros, of course, have longer and shorter maturities, with correspondingly lower and higher prices.

Fourth, EE bonds purchased after November 1982 pay a rate of interest that increases the longer you hold the bond. Most other zeros pay a fixed rate of interest determined by price at the time of purchase regardless of their maturity, although some original issue corporate zeros also pay indexed interest.

Today's EE bonds pay 4.35 percent six months after purchase to 7.26 percent after four years and six months; 7.51 percent from five to seven years after purchase; and 7.5 percent thereafter. Because of their upward-sliding interest schedule, EE bonds pay *more* than par value upon maturity: A $50 EE bond, for example, will be worth at least $52.22 at maturity.

There's another aspect to sliding EE bond interest: Held five years, EE bonds pay 85 percent of the average yield on five-year U.S. Treasury notes and are guaranteed to earn no less than 7.5 percent. Whenever average yields on five-year Treasuries exceed 7.5 percent, a $50 EE bond matures to more than $52.22—as will the other denominations. Therefore, with EE bonds, par value is an approximation, not a fixed figure.

Indexed yields on EE bonds have generated some confusion. If you read advertisements for EEs, they often encourage you to buy them with headlines like "EE Savings Bonds Purchased Today Yield 10.5 Percent. Interest Recalculated in Six Months." Yet if you read Treasury circulars pertaining to EE bonds, you'll discover that they yield only 4.35 percent during their first six months after purchase.

What really happens is that if you buy a EE bond today and redeem it in six months, it will pay 4.35 percent interest. However, if you hold it at least five years, the interest paid on the first six months of ownership will be recalculated to reflect 85 percent of the average five-year Treasury note yield. Therefore, the advertisement ought to read something like: "If you buy a EE Savings Bond today and hold it for five years, then five years from now the bond will be judged to have yielded 10.5 percent for the first six months you owned it."

The only way you know the maturity value of an EE bond for certain is to redeem it upon maturity. But if you want to track its yield while you own it, check the interest rate quotations published weekly in *The Wall Street Journal* or other financial publication.)

EE Savings Bonds differ from their descendants in other ways.

For one thing, EE bonds will never be worth less than purchase price even if cashed before maturity, nor will they ever be worth more than their scheduled value as determined by how long you've owned them. As we noted in the Introduction, zeros are the most volatile bonds because they're highly sensitive to interest rate changes. Because EE bond prices don't vary inversely with interest rates, they don't offer dramatic short-term gains, but by the same token they never suffer capital losses. Therefore, they're ideal for investors who demand capital stability.

Second, you may declare accreted interest from EE bonds as it accrues yearly, *or* you may postpone declaring interest until the bond matures or is cashed. Thus, EE bonds are an exception to tax laws that require you to pay tax on phantom income. Also, accreted interest from EE Savings Bonds is exempt from state, city, regional, and local taxes because EE bonds are U.S. government obligations. Deferral from federal tax along with exemption from state and local tax makes them attractive to high-bracket taxpayers.

Once you pick an option for declaring income from an EE bond you can't change it. However, you make the tax decision for each bond, so you may declare taxable interest on some EEs while deferring interest on others. Most investors enter higher tax brackets as they age. Consequently, you might find it useful to declare accreted interest on EE bonds purchased during lesser-taxed years and to defer taxation on EE bonds purchased when you enter higher brackets.

Third, EE bonds paying accreted interest may be exchanged for HH bonds paying coupon interest. The convertibility of EE bonds is such an attractive advantage for some investors that we have part of a chapter devoted to it and to a similar investment, the zero coupon convertible municipal bond. As we'll see, the convertibility feature makes it possible for you to have capital growth from EE bonds until you need current income.

But perhaps one of the greatest advantages of EE bonds is that their disadvantages really aren't disadvantages.

They're criticized for being registered and nontransferrable, meaning they can't be used for collateral or resold. On the other hand, registered securities are safe against theft and loss, and you can redeem the bonds at any bank or S&L.

Savings bonds do have impaired liquidity because you must hold them six months before you can cash them. For long-term investors, temporarily impaired liquidity is no consideration because they aren't turning investments around every six months. In any event, after six months the bonds are liquid at any teller's cage, and the offsetting advantage to impaired liquidity is stability of principal.

Each investor may purchase no more than $30,000 par value of EE bonds yearly. To get around this "disadvantage," you can buy $30,000 registered in your own name, your spouse can buy $30,000 in his or her name, the two of you can buy $30,000 in joint ownership, and each of your children can buy $30,000. These possibilities suggest that most investors can get all the EE bonds they want.

Another point often made against EE Savings Bonds is that they pay less interest than other types of zeros. That may be the case at present, but remember that every investment advantage "costs" something. EE bonds offer the formidable advantages of tax deferred interest, minimal purchase price, absence of commissions, federal government backing of principal and interest, ease of purchase, replacement without charge if lost, stolen, or mutilated, invulnerability to market loss, and total call protection before maturity. The "cost" of those advantages may be a bit of yield, but remember that EE bonds are indexed to five-year Treasury notes, so their yields are likely to be competitive.

You can buy savings bonds from several sources: in person at commercial banks, savings and loans, mutual savings associations, and Federal Reserve Banks; by sending a check to Bureau of the Public Debt in Washington, D.C. 20226; or through payroll savings at work and bond-a-month plans with banks. (If your company has no purchase plan, write Department A, U.S. Savings Bonds Division, Department of the Treasury, Washington, D.C. 20226, to start one.)

When you buy an EE bond, you must declare an owner of record. That can be yourself, yourself plus co-owner(s), or another person—for example, one of your children. The person who owns the bond is responsible for declaring or deferring federal income taxation.

Having outlined the features and advantages of EE bonds, let's look at some strategies you can follow in managing them.

We'll take only a brief look now, because we'll discuss some of their strategies more fully in later chapters, particularly when we discuss Uniform Gifts to Minors Accounts, convertible municipal zeros, and overall strategies for zero coupon bonds.

First, availability of EE bonds in small denominations means that you can acquire them painlessly without tilting your portfolio and without sacrificing current income needed for living expenses. In other words, they are very useful if you need long-term accumulations and can afford only modest sums to invest. In this regard, they may be preferable to zero coupon bond funds, which we'll examine in a later chapter.

Along with the advantages of long-term accumulations is the advantage of declaring interest or deferring interest. As we'll see in later chapters, EE bonds work best by declaring yearly interest when children own the bonds and by deferring interest when adults buy them.

Third, EE bonds fit exceptionally well with other types of zeros, and accordingly, they can be integral to managing a comprehensive portfolio of zero coupon securities, as we'll see in our chapter on managing a total investment in zero coupon bonds. EE bonds can be especially excellent as adjuncts to Individual Retirement Accounts, annuities, and employee investment plans as retirement-anticipation investments.

The first and original zero coupon bond may be the first one you should consider in constructing your portfolio of zeros. Stable, inexpensive, and offering special and useful features, the country's oldest zero coupon bond just might be the most important for your future. However, the U.S. Treasury has issued other types of zeros, and we need to take a look at those.

U.S. TREASURY BILLS

Treasury bills—more frequently shortened to "T-bills"—are short-term direct obligations of the U.S. government that mature in 13, 26, or 52 weeks. The term *bills* denotes the briefness of their maturity, as government notes usually mature in fewer than 10 years and government bonds usually mature in more than 10 years after they're issued.

Longtime favorites of money managers and conservative investors, T-bills are one of the safest investments and are often used in place of cash by many financial institutions. As direct obligations of Uncle Sam they are the nearest thing to default-proof, and their short-term maturities ensure minimal possibility of capital loss.

As we'll see in Chapter 7, T-bills are ideal zero coupon investments for the savings component of the portfolio because they're safe, liquid, and stable. Their one drawback is their high cost—at least $10,000.

Like all zeros, T-bills are issued at a discount from par, and interest is paid only when they mature. Under present law, interest is taxable in the year the bills mature, and you owe no tax on phantom interest while T-bills are maturing. As a direct obligation of the U.S. government, accreted interest on T-bills is exempt from state and local tax.

Whether you prefer 13-, 26-, or 52-week bills is largely a matter of preference. Most investors prefer 13-week bills because they give the greatest opportunity for reinvestment. The longer-running T-bills pay slightly higher interest, but many investors prefer the ready liquidity of shorter maturities. As we'll see in Chapter 7, T-bills can be bought from nearly any financial institution, including the Federal Reserve, and they can be sold easily prior to maturity if you need the cash.

STRIPS

In August 1984, the Department of the Treasury recognized the incredible popularity of derivative zeros (at that time more than $45 billion worth of Treasury bonds had been stripped to create derivative zeros) and undertook administrative actions that make it easier for financial institutions to create them. In February 1985, the Treasury's action resulted in the creation of STRIPS, which stands for Separate Trading of Registered Interest and Principal of Securities.

STRIPS were great for financial institutions, but they're a bane to financial writers because they're difficult to describe. In a nutshell, STRIPS aren't bonds; they're a blip on computer tape—a special designation on certain regular issues of Treasury bonds that enables them to be sold as regular Treasury bonds and also facilitates financial institutions' severing the coupon and interest payments to sell each separately.

The designation is called a CUSIP number, named for the American Banking Association Committee on Uniform Securities Identification Procedures (hence, CUSIP). Every security—stocks, government bonds, corporate bonds—has a distinct

TINTS - Shearson Lehman Bros.
(TReAsury INTerest)

CUSIP number by which it is identified. Under the STRIPS program, certain government bonds selected by the Treasury have multiple CUSIP numbers. With these specially identified bonds, the whole bond—principal and interest—has one CUSIP number, and each component of the bond—the principal and each coupon—also has its own CUSIP number. Having multiple CUSIP numbers makes it easier for financial institutions to resell severed interest and principal payments because each already has a preestablished CUSIP number.

The problem is further complicated because STRIPS are direct issues of the U.S government, but they aren't issued by the U.S. government, and private investors can't buy them directly. They're for sale only to financial institutions that have book-entry securities accounts with the Federal Reserve. In other words, STRIPS exist on computer tape only, and they may be purchased only by financial institutions that are on file with the Fed's computer.

However, financial institutions can resell their purchases of STRIPS to individual investors under their trade names. For instance, Shearson Lehman Brothers, the international brokerage institution, sells STRIPs under its trade name TINTS, standing for Treasury Interest. As other financial institutions purchase quantities of STRIPS, they'll no doubt resell them under their trademarked names. So someday you may go to Merrill Lynch to buy TIGRs and take home a briefcase full of STRIPS without knowing it.

For our purposes, we can regard STRIPS exactly as we regard any other derivative zero, because that's the way you'll end up with them. They work exactly like the derivative zeros we discussed in Chapter 2, and the same circumstances regarding maturity, safety, commissions, and other features apply. So, henceforth, when we refer to derivative zeros, bear in mind that we're also talking about STRIPS, even though they're a little different from other derivative zeros as far as their origin is concerned.

STRIPS produce phantom taxable interest yearly, so if you hold them outside IRAs and Keogh Plans you'll be expected to declare a portion of accreted interest each year. However, phantom interest on STRIPS is exempt from state and local tax, which isn't the case with other felines. The formula is the one used for calculating compound accreted interest, which is the final formula covered in Chapter 1. Fortunately, IRS Publication

1212 shows the phantom taxable interest due on STRIPS held outside IRAs and Keoghs.

FEDERAL NATIONAL MORTGAGE ASSOCIATION ZEROS

The Federal National Mortgage Association, better known as "Fannie Mae," has issued several categories of indebtedness under its charter as a taxpaying, shareholder-owned corporation whose assets (more than $90 billion in home mortgages) make it the third largest corporation in the United States. Although Fannie Mae is always adamant in declaring that its debt is not a direct obligation of the U.S. government, most investors regard its obligations on a plane with government securities, and Fannie Mae debt is rated AAA.

Fannie Mae's best-known investment is a pass-through bond that represents interest and principal payments on millions of mortgages. However, with the advent of zero coupon investments, Fannie Mae has begun to issue some of those, too.

In late 1984, Salomon Bros. and Nomura Securities International underwrote a $6.7 billion offering of Federal National Mortgage Association Zero Coupon Subordinated Capital Debentures maturing in 2019. Perhaps by this time Fannie Mae will have issued another series of what it calls Capital Debentures, which is its trade name for its zero coupon debt.

These are original issue zeros from a private corporation that is presumed to be able to call upon the backing of the U.S. government. Consequently, they're regarded as a close proxy for CATS and TIGRs and other derivative zeros even though they are not, strictly speaking, backed by the government. Like all zeros, they're sold at deep discounts from par, but the minimum face value you can buy is $5,000. When first issued, Capital Debentures could be purchased only from the underwriters, but Fannie Mae intends to apply for listing on the New York Bond Exchange. Assuming that the listing is approved, Fannie Mae's Capital Debentures can be bought and sold like any publicly traded zero, and, as a zero coupon investor, you can investigate them for your portfolio.

COLLATERALIZED MORTGAGE OBLIGATIONS

A security similar to the Fannie Mae Capital Debentures, Collateralized Mortgage Obligations (CMOs) are a recent financial innovation that takes pools of private mortgages and restructures them. However, CMOs can have a variety of issuers, which means you'll have to investigate their investment merits according to techniques we'll discuss under corporate original issue zeros.

CMOs are akin to derivative zeros in that they are created from another type of security called a mortgage-backed passthrough. Most such securities pay conventional coupon interest at regular intervals, usually monthly rather than semiannually. However, the final class of CMOs—that is, the last security in the series issued—is called a Z-piece, and it is sold like a conventional zero at a deep original issue discount.

The Z-piece (the Z presumably stands for zero) pays accreted interest only upon maturity. Consequently, it can be issued and purchased just like any of the zeros we've discussed. Remember, however, that there is as yet no public market for this type of zero. Markets will be maintained by the issuer, presumably a bank, mortgage institution, or savings and loan. They may not be as liquid as other types of zeros.

ZERO COUPON CORPORATE BONDS

Following the advent of derivative zeros, corporations were quick to seize upon their advantages and popularity by issuing their own original issue zeros. In the case of corporations, there was a special attraction for hopping on the zero bandwagon: Whereas private investors must usually declare phantom taxable interest yearly even though they don't receive it until maturity, corporations may claim a tax deduction for phantom interest as if they'd actually paid it.

Although the dollar volume of corporate zeros is small when compared to the multibillions of derivative and municipal zeros, a growing number of corporations have issued zero coupon debt. If you go through the New York Bond Exchange Listings in *The Wall Street Journal* or in your daily newspaper, you'll see that corporations like Allied-Signal, Bank of America, Cities Service, General Mills, Merrill Lynch (its own corporate debt, not its TIGRs), and others have zeros listed on public exchanges. As we'd expect, this corporate debt features a range of maturities and prices. The American Exchange bond market also trades a few corporate zeros.

Again, these zeros operate just like all the other zeros we've studied, except that they are backed only by the profitability of the issuing corporation. Just like derivative zeros, their principal characteristics are price, yield, par value, and maturity. Quotations for corporate zeros are translated in the manner we learned in Chapter 1, and their yields are also calculated by the method described there.

Corporate zeros do have a few singular characteristics, however. Some corporate zeros feature sliding interest rates geared to the profitability of the issuer or to an index such as the consumer price index or the rates on Treasury bonds. Although nearly all corporate zeros feature $1,000 par, indexed corporate zeros may mature to more than $1,000.

Further, a special type of corporate zero is convertible into the common or preferred stock of the issuer. Convertibility gives investors the chance to profit from price appreciation of the underlying shares as well as price appreciation from decreases in interest rates. We'll look further at convertible corporate zeros in a special chapter devoted to convertibles.

Because they aren't underpinned by government securities, corporate zeros are vulnerable to default. Furthermore, their prices are influenced by the issuer's profitability and by the general course of interest rates. That combination makes them less secure and more volatile than derivative zeros.

Because of these twin drawbacks, corporate zeros present a more complicated problem in investment analysis. A basic investment text can give you a thumbnail course in debt analysis, but here are a few guidelines you can use in analyzing corporate zeros.

First, check the subordination of zeros to other debt of the issuer. Corporate bonds (actually, most are debentures) have junior and senior issues. As the terms imply, senior debt receives preference for payment if the corporation goes under. Junior debt is paid after senior debt; most corporations have several layers of junior debt. Most—but not all—corporate zeros are junior debt. That doesn't mean you should avoid them; it merely means you need to look at the next step in the analysis.

That next step is to check the coverage ratios. This information is available from Standard & Poor's and Moody's guides to corporate debt, from Value Line stock guides, and from your broker. A coverage ratio measures the relationship of corporate assets to corporate debt—not only physical assets like plant and equipment but also cash and near-cash assets like T-bills held in the corporate coffers. Coverage ratios give you an idea of how easily a corporation could cover its debt if it had to. Generally, a 1:1 ratio is acceptable, although many investors want a 2:1 ratio. A 2:1 ratio means that two dollars of corporate assets or cash cover each dollar of debt.

As a form of financial shorthand, you can ask what the corporation's debt rating is. As we've mentioned, independent rating agencies like Moody's and Standard & Poor's rate corporate debt for assurance against default. Given so many attractive derivative zeros available, there's no reason to accept less than A-rated corporate zeros. The slight advantage in yield over derivative zeros probably won't compensate for increased risk of default.

As we'll see in later chapters, corporate zeros can be used in the same strategies as derivative and other original issue zeros. They can be purchased for a buy-and-hold strategy, bought for aggressive gains, included in IRAs and Keoghs, and added to Uniform Gifts to Minors Accounts. As a generality, however, derivative zeros offer a wider range of maturities than do corporate zeros, and they are not influenced by profitability considerations. These two facts often compel many investors to prefer derivatives over corporates.

ZERO COUPON CERTIFICATES OF DEPOSIT

A good thing draws a following, and as has been so often the case during the past decade, banks and S&Ls have been followers in financial markets rather than leaders. Nonetheless, they have followed a good lead in offering certificates of deposit in zero coupon form.

Like conventional interest-paying CDs, zero CDs are direct issues of the sponsoring depositary. They are sold at discounts from par to mature in a fixed number of years. Generally, the disadvantage of zero CDs is their limited range of maturities. With few exceptions, zero CDs are offered in five-year maturities at a price of $500 per $1,000 par value and 12-year maturities for a price of $250.

However, some depositaries with a national customer base have expanded their range of maturities and par values. It is possible to buy zero CDs from a few depositaries in maturities of 1, 5, 10, 12, and 20 years at yields that increase with the term of deposit. Par values of these broader-access zero CDs range from $1,000 to $100,000, and information about them occasionally appears in *The Wall Street Journal* and other financial publications.

Customarily, only the largest denominations of zero CDs are liquid. Zero CDs of less than $100,000 par value usually aren't traded in public or private markets, and if you sell them prior to maturity you'll pay interest penalties. Therefore, most zero CDs aren't suitable for anything other than a buy-and-hold strategy.

You can hold zero CDs as you would any other CD, and interest will be taxable yearly or upon maturity, depending upon when the CD was issued. Zero CDs issued after 1984 are taxable yearly according to the compound interest method. Zero CDs held in IRAs and Keoghs compound tax-deferred until you make withdrawals from your account.

In addition to zero CDs purchased directly from a sponsoring depositary, you can purchase reoffered CDs from banks and brokerages that purchase "jumbo CDs" from the original issuers and break them into smaller denominations for resale. The brokerage's procedure is essentially the same as for reoffering T-bonds as CATS and TIGRs.

You purchase these derivative CDs from the offering brokerage for prices and yields and par values determined by the offering. Generally, original issue CDs and reoffered CDs carry FDIC or FSLIC insurance, so they're highly secure against default. Sometimes the offering brokerage will make a market in its reoffered CDs, which means you have some liquidity without interest penalties. However, if you sell a zero CD back to the sponsor, you'll be at its mercy for the price you receive. Your sales price could be less than your purchase price, especially for longer maturities.

Zero CDs carry the advantages of known purchase price, known yield, and known accumulations that are found in other zeros. They are also immune to price fluctuations, which makes them desirable for conservative investors, and they require no commission for purchase.

These advantages aside, zero coupon CDs are not generally useful by themselves. Excluding the jumbo denominations of $100,000, zero CDs are usually illiquid before maturity. Their illiquidity makes them useful only as a kind of hands-off extension of your savings component. However, zero CDs can be excellent adjuncts to other zero coupon investments.

Say, for example, that you can't find an attractive corporate or derivative zero with a 12-year maturity. You could select a zero CD from a bank or brokerage and blend it in with your other holdings of zeros. As we'll see later, blending different types of zeros provides optimum usefulness and balance in your portfolio.

SUMMARY

From CATS and TIGRs and other derivative zeros we've arrived at a broader spectrum of zero coupon investments. Ranging from EE Savings Bonds through STRIPS and Fannie Maes and corporate zeros and zero coupon CDs, the zero coupon craze has permeated financial markets. There is scarcely a debtor in the economy who hasn't issued some form of zero coupon security.

What's even better from the viewpoint of the private investor, issuers have become more innovative in the types of zeros they're offering to the public. The next chapter is devoted to another popular original issue zero, the zero coupon municipal bond. After we look at municipal zeros, we'll examine two other types of zero coupon investments, namely convertible zeros and zero coupon funds.

Now that we've examined the basics of the fundamental types of zeros available, let's take a look at the innovative advancements recently created in the zero coupon market.

4

Zero Coupon Municipal Bonds

For some investors, federally taxable phantom yearly interest is a great drawback to owning zeros outside tax-deferred IRAs and Keogh Accounts. But that's no reason to avoid zeros altogether, for zero coupon municipal bonds provide the same advantages as other zeros as well as exemption from federal taxation. As we'll see, zero municipals can be very useful even for investors in low tax brackets, and they might even be more attractive than zeros in your IRA and Keogh Accounts.

Municipal zeros work exactly like their fully taxable brethren. However, the difference between their purchase price and par value is federally untaxed accreted interest. Unlike the situation with corporate and derivative zeros, Uncle Sam doesn't expect to see phantom interest on municipal zeros declared yearly on your federal 1040. Your state may tax accreted interest, but we'll cover that later.

Conventionally, municipal securities are considered suitable only for investors in 30-percent-plus tax brackets. Many people argue that reducing the highest tax brackets would destroy the attractiveness of municipals for many investors. We, however, need not be so conventional in our thinking. Regardless of their tax brackets, many investors can benefit from municipal zeros in a number of ways.

ADVANTAGES OF MUNICIPAL ZEROS

First, many stock brokers report that investors are forsaking growth-oriented common stocks for municipal zeros because zeros' accumulations and tax advantages make stocks uncompetitive.

As an example, in early 1986 municipal zeros maturing in 1990 were selling for about $650 per $1,000 face value. A $6,500 investment would produce $3,500 federally untaxed in five years. You have no way of knowing what an investment in stocks will be worth in five years, so the predictability of municipal zeros (in fact, of all zeros) is one immediate advantage over growth stocks.

In addition, stocks are subject to capital gains taxation, which municipal zeros avoid if you hold them to maturity. Even if you have a stock that performs as well as a zero over five years, it has to perform even better to produce an equivalent after-tax return. What's more, when zeros with 15- to 20-year maturities produce federally untaxed returns of 10 to 12 percent, as they have in the recent past, a portfolio of long-term growth stocks would really have to go some in order to produce the equivalent after-tax returns.

Second, aggressive investors find that municipal zeros can be bought and sold for speculative returns without many of the risks associated with many aggressive investments. We'll look at aggressive management of zeros in their own section later, but we can scan the concept briefly now.

With long-term zeros' low prices, an aggressive investor could buy a trading lot—about $100,000 to $250,000 face value—of the Sam Rayburn zeros mentioned in Chapter 1 for a bit more than $18,000. When interest rates decline, these long-term issues will produce sharp capital appreciation. The aggressive investor can sell the zeros rather than hold them to maturity, take federally taxed capital gains, and reinvest elsewhere.

If interest rates don't fall, producing aggressive gains, investors can hold the zeros, receiving federally untaxed growth until price movements produce the desired return. Even if the investor ends up holding the zeros until they mature, he or she still has returns that probably will beat an aggressive strategy from stocks on an after-tax basis.

Third, many advisors earnestly recommend that every working American open an IRA, yet few realize that municipal zeros might produce greater total returns than IRAs, even considering the tax write-off for an IRA contribution.

For instance, the CATS of 2011 in Chapter 1 were selling for about $100 apiece. For an investment of $2,000, disregarding commissions, we could have bought 20 CATS for an IRA, and we would receive $20,000 when they mature. The accreted interest from the CATS would be tax-deferred in an IRA, but when we begin receiving income from the IRAs we would be fully taxed on distributions.

At the same time the CATS were selling for $100, the Sam Rayburn public power municipal zeros maturing in 2012 were selling for $73.79. An investment of $1,844.75 (requiring no commissions because they were purchased directly from a sponsoring dealer) would grow to $25,000 with *no* federal tax liability. The zero municipal generates none of the tax offsets of the CATS in an IRA, but, on an investment-versus-investment basis, the munies cost $150 less, generate $5,000 more in accreted interest, and all of it is federally untaxed as opposed to tax deferred. If the IRA was a good investment, municipal zeros are probably a better investment, because they're also liquid without tax penalties, which isn't true of IRAs and Keoghs.

Even better, you don't have to choose municipal zeros over other zeros. You can have both: the tax-deferred accumulations of zeros in IRAs and the federally untaxed accumulations of municipal zeros in other accounts. (Do not buy municipal zeros for an IRA or Keogh. When you begin receiving distributions from tax-deferred retirement accounts, they'll be fully taxed. You'll forfeit municipal zeros' federally untaxed returns by holding them in IRAs and Keoghs.) There are some excellent reasons why you'd want to match different types of zeros, and we'll cover those reasons in our section on investment strategies.

SPECIAL CONSIDERATIONS OF MUNICIPAL ZEROS

Advantageous as municipal zeros are, you need to be aware of special considerations governing your choices of these issues.

First, protection against default is greater when the zeros are "general obligations" of an issuing state and greatest when zeros are "insured" by independent agencies.

In general, municipal zeros are of two types: general obligations and project bonds. A general obligation zero is backed by the taxing power of the state issuing it. Occasionally, zeros are backed by lesser tax authorities—a city or a regional tax agency—or by interest to be paid from certain types of taxes or fees, such as school levies or highway tolls.

Project bonds are backed by revenues expected from such

municipal projects as a university dormitory, housing construction, a sewer system, a public power project, or a highway authority, among others. Project zeros are better known by their financially correct names specified in their issuing prospectus, but they are similar in that accreted interest is paid from revenues financed by the borrowed capital. Because these projects have to make money before you're paid, they are generally less secure than zeros that have interest paid by the taxing authority of the state.

Assurance against default is measured by independent rating agencies like Moody's or Standard & Poor's, which assign grades specifying the safety of the issue. These agencies study the debt coverage and financial standing of the issuing state or authority and encapsulate their findings in financial shorthand that reflects their analysis. The highest rating is AAA, which indicates maximum assurance against default, at least in the opinion of the rater. Subordinate ratings, like AA or A, indicate high quality issues with slightly less assurance against default, and BBB is the lowest rating for "investment grade" securities. There are so many good-quality municipal zeros that there's really no reason to accept less than an A rating. For long-term zeros, those of 15 years or more, most investors will accept nothing lower than AA.

The maximum assurance against default is afforded by "insured" municipals, which carry a AAA rating because of their "insurance." Insured municipals are doubly and triply backed. If, for some reason, a revenue or taxing authority is unable to pay accreted interest, insured municipals can call upon the promise of agencies like the Municipal Bond Insurance Association and others to make good upon payment of interest and repayment of principal. Because of their advanced assurance against default, AAA insured municipals usually carry lower interest than lesser-rated zeros. However, most investors gladly sacrifice a point or less in yield for greater assurance against default, particularly when investing long term.

There are other circumstances that will merit a AAA rating besides the innate quality of the issuer and insurance backing. For example, some zeros are "escrowed," which means that the issuer has purchased U.S. government bonds or has deposited compensating funds in a bank to serve as collateral against the zero coupon debt. So long as the issue is AAA, it really doesn't matter why, because you're buying the highest quality paper.

What does matter—and a great deal—is "call protection," a subject that we introduced earlier. Municipal issues are often "callable" at a certain point in their lives, meaning that the issuer can redeem this debt before it matures. Callable zeros can be an advantage or a disadvantage, depending upon the "price to call" and "yield to call."

If a municipal zero is callable, it will be annotated with a "c" in its prospectus or in investment literature from a broker. The literature will also specify a date of callability, a price at which the issue can be redeemed, and sometimes a yield to that date. The price will be either a percentage of par or will be a dollar amount.

For example, let's say that a zero matures in the year 2000 with a yield to maturity of 10 percent, and further information indicates "c1995 at 102 ytc 10.12." This means that beginning in 1995 and any time thereafter the zero can be called back from purchasers at a price of 102 percent of par for a yield to call (ytc) of 10.12 percent. For the most part, investors would say this is excellent "callability," for the zero produces greater price and yield than if it were held to maturity. However, such isn't always the case, for some zeros produce less because of their call features.

For example, zeros with features otherwise identical to the example above might contain provisions like "c1990 at 83.95." This means that the zero is callable in 1990 rather than 1995, and in this case a price is specified of $83.95 per $100, or $839.50 per $1,000 of par value. No yield to call is given, so you have to ask—pointedly—what it is. In this example, if the zero is called in 1990 you receive a price of $839.50 for each bond you own. That clearly is less than par value, and in this particular case the yield to call is also less—about 8.2 percent, based upon information in the prospectus.

Because an issue is callable doesn't mean that your particular zeros will be called. Sometimes an entire issue is callable, or sometimes an issue will feature "serial call," which means that some bonds in the total issue can be or will be redeemed at earlier or later times than other bonds in the issue. Sometimes an issuer fully intends to call its zeros, and other times the issuer merely wants the option of calling them if it's an advantage to do so.

There is one important phrase you need to master in considering call features and their influence upon municipal zeros.

The phrase is *ask about them.* Circumstance by circumstance, callability can be a great advantage or disadvantage for you.

Apart from quality and call features, the most important consideration for municipal zeros is their maturity. If you intend to trade zeros aggressively, you'll probably be interested only in the longest maturities, for they produce the greatest price fluctuations as interest rates fall. If you're buying municipal zeros for a specific purpose—as an adjunct to your IRA, for instance—then you'll probably want issues that mature during years that coincide with your anticipated retirement. We'll look at strategies for managing municipal zeros in a later chapter.

Zero municipals are exempt from federal tax, and some states don't tax accreted interest on their own bonds or on certain types of issues. If you're a resident of such a state or are holding untaxed issues, you pay no state or federal tax on your zeros. However, most states tax accreted interest in one of two ways. First, your state might expect you to declare phantom accreted interest yearly. Second, your state might require you to declare accreted interest when the bond matures or when you sell it.

If your state taxes accreted interest yearly, your state internal revenue service will provide you a formula for determining that interest. Request the formula from your state IRS, or ask your broker for it. Generally, the formula for determining taxable interest in your state will be par value minus purchase price divided by years to maturity. This is the straight line method of calculating phantom taxable interest, and it's still in wide use for zero coupon municipals. In our example, we'll use the straight line method, but your state might require the compound interest method.

To illustrate, say you purchased $100,000 of municipal zeros for $10,000 and they mature in 20 years. Your calculation would be

$$\frac{\$100,000 - \$10,000}{20} = \frac{\$90,000}{20} = \$4,500$$

If your state taxes accreted interest yearly according to the straight line method, your state internal revenue service would expect you to declare $4,500 as taxable received interest each year that you owned the zeros. If your state taxes the accreted interest when the zeros mature, you would owe tax on $90,000 of received interest at the end of 20 years. If your state does not tax interest on this particular zero or on any municipal zero of its own origin, you owe no tax to the state or the federal government. However, check to see if city or regional taxes might apply.

If you sell zeros before maturity, you'll possibly be liable for federal and state capital gains tax, assuming the zero produced a gain, and tax on accreted interest at the date of sale. Typically, capital gains from zeros are defined as sale price minus purchase price minus phantom interest presumed to have been received.

For example, say that you sold the zeros in the example above for $15,000 after owning them for one year. Sale price of $15,000 minus purchase price of $10,000 leaves $5,000. However, when you sell a municipal zero prior to maturity, a portion of the gain is usually presumed to be payment for accreted interest—in this case, $4,500. Therefore, our $5,000 total return is $4,500 in interest and $500 in capital gain. The federal government won't tax the interest portion of the total return; your state government might or might not, depending upon whether it taxes municipal interest; both will tax the capital gain.

Selling municipal zeros at a loss is a more complicated problem if your state taxes accreted interest. Even though you can declare the loss on your federal tax return, thereby aiding your state and federal tax burden, your state IRS might still expect you to declare phantom interest as if you'd actually received it. The unreceived gain can wipe out the actual loss.

To alter our example slightly, let's say you bought the municipal zeros for $10,000 and sold them a year later for $8,000. You have a capital loss of $2,000. You can declare that loss on your federal 1040. Because states usually determine taxable income on the basis of a federal tax return, the capital loss can help with your state tax liability. However, if your state taxes accreted interest, you are also expected to declare it as received interest even though it never materialized in your checkbook. In our example, you still have $4,500 of phantom interest to declare, even though you never received it and have no prospect of receiving it.

However, state laws are far from uniform. Under some circumstances—difference in state law, differences in treatment of zeros issued at different times—the capital loss might be a full capital loss without obligation to declare phantom interest. If you're going to sell municipal zeros before maturity, consult qualified tax counsel before executing the transaction.

Of course, your situation is improved if your state doesn't tax municipal interest in general or on particular issues of zeros. But most taxpayers will prefer to avoid tax—to say nothing of mathematical—problems by holding municipal zeros to maturity. Before selling any zero coupon investment, whether at a loss or a gain, consult a reputable authority to determine the tax consequences.

SUMMARY

Zero coupon municipal securities can be very advantageous to all types of investors, not merely to the highest taxed. By understanding the importance of security, call provisions, interest backing, and tax consequences, you can maximize the advantages of these securities.

We've looked briefly at two strategies for zeros—buying them to hold and buying them for capital gains—and we'll look more deeply into these strategies in Part Two. What's more, there are other types of zeros that can be highly useful in a comprehensive portfolio. For example, we'll examine convertible zeros, including convertible municipals, in the next chapter, when we'll see how to take advantage of issues that grow as zeros and then become current-income bonds. We'll also study municipal securities trusts and mutual funds that offer the advantages of zeros through indirect investment.

Whatever your preference or needs, zero coupon investments can be wise additions to your portfolio. Either by themselves or as companions to other types of zero coupon securities, municipal zeros can add balance, dimension, and profits to your investment program.

5

Convertible Zero Coupon Bonds

One frequent criticism of zero coupon bonds is that they are useless to investors who need current income. That's a little like complaining that pigs don't walk around with knives and forks, inquiring if you're hungry. However, there are two types of zeros that are useful to investors who want to mate the long-term accumulations of zeros with current income later. Generally, such investors are in higher tax brackets, around age 55, and anticipate retiring in 10 years, and the zeros of particular interest to them are convertible municipal bonds and EE Savings Bonds.

Most investors are familiar with corporate convertible bonds, named "convertibles" because they permit you to exchange them for the company's common or preferred stock. Convertible municipals are slightly different. They're zero coupon bonds that convert into income bonds 10 to 12 years after issue. Consequently, they feature a decade or so of capital growth followed by a decade of current income, and that's ideal for investors who might otherwise be attracted to annuities, which provide the same investment characteristics.

To study an example of municipal zero convertibles, let's consider the Broward County Florida Housing Finance Authority issue.

Until July 1997, these are zero coupon municipal bonds earning interest as the difference between price paid (about

$320 per bond) and par value of $1,000. Beginning in mid-1997, however, they convert to coupon-paying bonds maturing in 2007 and yielding 10 percent.

In other words, $3,200 invested today grows to $10,000 in 1997—a federally untaxed gain of about $6,800 on a yield-to-conversion of 10 percent. From 1997 until 2007, these bonds pay $1,000 in federally untaxed annual interest—$10,000 over 10 years. In 2007 when the bonds mature, you receive the $10,000 par value to spend or to reinvest. In case you don't have your pocket calculator handy, you started out with $3,200 and ended up with $20,000, federally untaxed. All of the present convertible municipals are investment-grade obligations rated A or better, so you can invest long-term with greater confidence.

ADVANTAGES AND DISADVANTAGES

It should be easy to see why convertible municipal zeros are attractive investments. Apart from their built-in growth and income, they're safe, predictable, and profitable in addition to being federally untaxed. Consequently, they may be the optimum investment of their type, and more sophisticated investors can see right away that they're an excellent adjunct to zeros in an Individual Retirement Account. More about that in a later chapter, however.

In order to profit from the advantages of municipal convertibles, you have to accept two possible disadvantages. Some convertible municipals are callable before maturity, so you have to ask about yield-to-call as well as yield-to-conversion, although most convertibles have excellent call protection. Also, convertibles fluctuate in price like any publicly traded instrument. If you sell them before maturity, a capital loss is possible, but so is a capital gain.

Although exempt from federal taxation throughout their lives, municipal convertibles might be subject to state tax where you live. While the convertible is a zero coupon bond, some states expect you to declare accreted interest yearly, whereas others permit you to postpone tax until the bond converts to a current-income bond. When the bond starts paying coupon interest, your state might tax that interest as current income. However, some states don't tax interest on their own securities even if they tax interest on bonds from other states. Ask your broker about tax on municipal convertibles where you live.

One of the best sources of zero convertibles is Gabriele, Hueglin & Cashman, Inc., at 44 Wall Street in New York City. [(800) 422-7435 outside New York State or (212) 422-1700 in state.] As a substantial underwriter of convertibles, Gabriele has a large inventory and makes its money on basis pricing, not commissions. Other brokerages handle convertible municipals, and whether they charge commissions depends upon whether they're holding convertibles in inventory or must obtain them from another brokerage.

Convertible municipals are sold under several names— GAINS (Growth and Income Securities), PACS (Principal Appreciation Conversion Securities), FIGS (Future Income and Growth Securities), TEDIS (Tax Exempt Discount and Income Securities), BIGS (Bond Income and Growth Securities)—but they're all fundamentally the same. So long as you understand the basic concept underlying convertible municipal zeros and can ask the pertinent questions we outlined in the chapter on zero coupon municipal bonds, it doesn't matter what they're named.

CONVENIENCE IN ARRANGING CURRENT INCOME

The convertible municipal bond is a major new innovation in the development of zero coupon products, and it overcomes a frequent criticism of zeros—inability to provide current income. As a highly advantaged product for investors needing current income for their portfolios, municipal zeros will surely attract attention from knowledgeable investors.

Zero coupon municipals are a particularly attractive buy for today's investors. As of mid-1986, these are unfamiliar to many investors who are otherwise conversant with municipal zeros, so their prices are a bit lower and their yields a bit higher than are common with municipals of similar maturity and quality. Their unfamiliarity creates a market aberration that astute investors will want to take advantage of quickly, as it probably will fade as investors catch on to the attractiveness of an investment that provides capital accumulations now and current income later.

In Chapter 8, we discuss the current income component of the portfolio, and we'll see how investors can serialize the maturities of other zero coupon investments to provide a source of current income when a carefully structured assortment of zeros pays out par values. Although serializing maturities is an excellent and underutilized way to structure zeros for income and to overcome one failing of zero coupon investments, convertible municipals handle both problems simultaneously and provide federally untaxed interest and a lump sum payment that can be reinvested for continuing gains. These advantages are tailor-made for middle-aged investors who are probably in the highest tax brackets of their careers and who will need both current income in the 10 years that municipal zeros convert to coupon-paying bonds and reinvestable capital later.

OTHER PARTICULARS

However, you don't have to be 50 to 55 years old before convertible municipals can be useful to you, nor must you regard them only as substitutes for an annuity. They're excellent for highly taxed investors of any age, and their federally untaxed coupon yield—averaging 10 percent for the current crop of municipal convertibles—is competitive anytime.

Generally speaking, there's no minimum purchase amount, although most brokerages expect you to buy at least $10,000 face value of any municipal bond and some will require a minimum of $25,000 face value. And that's *face value,* not cash outlay. At their modest prices, convertibles are easily affordable, even for very large face values.

If a minimum investment of $3,000 to $5,000 does present a problem, however, there's a cheaper and more accessible type of convertible zero: our old acquaintance the EE Savings Bond. It, too, can be a useful retirement-anticipation investment, provided you have patience and the will to manage your bonds. (If you're not conversant with the characteristics and advantages of EE bonds, refer to Chapter 3.)

EE SAVINGS BONDS AND HH SAVINGS BONDS

Although EE bonds pay accreted interest like all zeros, they can be exchanged for HH Savings Bonds paying coupon interest. By exchanging EE for HH bonds, you can have capital growth followed by current income, and you can also defer federal taxes.

HH

Special TAX Deferral w·Th HH Bonds ?.

Like conventional corporate or municipal bonds, HH bonds make twice-yearly payments until the bond matures 10 years after purchase. HH bonds purchased after November 1982 pay 7½ percent coupon interest based on par values of $500, $1,000, $5,000, and $10,000. A $10,000 HH bond, for instance, will pay $750 in twice-yearly checks of $375. Even if you redeem an HH bond before maturity, it will never be worth less than par value, and that's a major advantage of HH bonds over all other corporate, municipal, or government bonds.

However, converting EE bonds for HH bonds presents a logistical problem. You have to bundle up all of your EE bonds and deliver them to a Federal Reserve Bank or branch or to the Bureau of the Public Debt in Washington, D.C. 20226, or in Parkersburg, West Virginia 26101. When you convert EE for HH bonds, the EEs must be at least six months old and must have accreted to at least $500, the minimum par value for HH bonds.

In our chapter on zero coupon bonds and Uniform Gifts to Minors Accounts, we outline strategies for using EE bonds in building estates for children. We note there that the best strategy is to declare EE bond accreted interest yearly so that children can escape taxation. However, your tax bracket will be higher than your children's, so you want to defer having to declare EE bond interest until you're retired and probably in a lesser tax bracket. If you convert EE bonds for HH bonds, you need not declare accrued EE bond interest until you redeem the HH bond or it matures 10 years after purchase. This special tax-deferral feature means you can defer taxes on your EE bonds for 20 years if you choose.

Exchange of EE bonds for HH bonds works effectively whether you collect small-denomination EEs over many years, investing as little as $25 at a time, or if you invest a single sum in large-denomination EEs. Unfortunately, EE bonds mature in 10 years, which means that the easiest way to manage their conversion feature is to buy them 10 years before you expect to retire. If you start buying EEs earlier, you run into the problem of staggered maturities and end up having to declare deferred EE bond interest when you're in the highest tax brackets of your career. That's both annoying and inefficient, but it's not the end of the world. Still, one of our goals is to manage zero coupon bonds efficiently and easily, so let's outline the optimum scenario.

CONVERTING EE TO HH BONDS UPON RETIREMENT

Let's say you expect to retire in 10 years—making you about 55 years old—and you have $500 to invest. Here's what you can do.

Buy a $1,000 EE bond and elect to defer interest. Put the bond in a drawer or safety deposit box until it matures in 10 years.

On that date, when you're ready to retire, your initial $500 investment will have grown to at least $1,000 if your EE bond paid only the minimum $7\frac{1}{2}$ percent interest. If average yields on five-year Treasuries exceeded $7\frac{1}{2}$ percent during your holding period, your EE bonds will have grown to more than $1,000 and would be convertible for HH bonds of greater par value.

Convert the EE bond to HH bond in the manner described. By converting, you continue to defer tax on the accreted EE bond interest unless you elect to pay the tax on accreted interest during the year of conversion.

Your HH bond will pay $75 interest yearly ($37.50 every six months) for 10 years. Again, we've assumed only that your EE bond accreted to $1,000. In fact, your exchanged EE may have been worth more than $1,000 and perhaps enough to convert it for more than one $1,000 HH bond. If that's the case, you'll be receiving more than $75 yearly coupon interest. Coupon interest from the HH bond is federally taxable, but it is exempt from state and local taxes.

Draw interest on your HH bond for 10 years. When the bond finally matures, you must declare all accreted EE bond interest as federally taxable if you had elected to defer it earlier. However, you can reinvest the par value of your HH bonds for continuing returns.

In sum, you invested $500 and over 20 years you received at least $1,750 in accreted and coupon interest on which you paid no state or local taxes and could have deferred some federal taxes. That's more than three times your money. Obviously, if you could have invested more—say $5,000 instead of $500—you could multiply all of these results by a factor of 10. But if you can afford to invest more, you'll want to consider zero coupon municipal convertibles to capture their advantages. And if you're interested in corporate zeros, you might also want to consider the newest innovation in zero coupon investments, the corporate convertible zero.

CORPORATE CONVERTIBLE ZEROS

Late 1985 saw the advent of a few zero coupon corporate debentures that offer conversion into stock of the issuing corporation just like the conventional coupon-paying corporate convertible. Although corporate convertible zeros don't convert directly into income producers like municipal convertibles, they offer a number of attractions.

First, they offer the standard advantages of zeros—low price, known accumulations, fixed reinvestment returns, and a defined time horizon.

Second, they offer the prospect of price appreciation not only from declines in interest rates but also from appreciation of the underlying stock.

Third, many corporate convertible zeros have "put features," which entitle you to sell the bond back to the issuer at a specified price after a specified date. Put features, which are also available on some zero coupon and conventional municipal bonds, minimize your downside risk.

Fourth, if you convert your corporate convertible zero into stock of the issuing corporation, you may receive some dividend income from the shares of stock you received from converting the zero.

There are several key terms you should be familiar with if you're considering corporate convertible zeros.

Of course, all the terms we've covered with reference to zero coupon investments generally apply to corporate zero convertibles—yield to maturity, quality rating, par value, maturity, callability, and yield to call. To these terms we add some special vocabulary relating to conversion features.

"Conversion ratio" is the number of shares you receive when you trade the corporate convertible zero into stock (either common or preferred stock, depending upon the issuing corporation). This figure is revealed in the bond covenant or prospectus. It's important because it tells you how many shares of stock you'll receive if you convert the bond to shares.

"Stock price at conversion" is the purchase price of the convertible corporate zero divided by the conversion ratio. For instance, if you purchased the corporate convertible for $200 and the conversion ratio is five, the effective purchase price of the underlying stock is about $40. This figure is important because it shows how much the stock will have to appreciate before it's advantageous to convert the zero into stock.

"Conversion value" is the *current* market value of the number of shares you can receive by converting the zero into stock. To find conversion value, multiply the conversion ratio by the *current* stock price. For example, if the conversion ratio is 10 and the stock is selling at $20 per share, the conversion value is $200. This figure is important because it tells you how much the bond is worth today, when you're buying the bond, as measured by the price of the stock it's convertible into.

Let's put these terms to work in an actual example and see how we'd use them. In late 1985, Merrill Lynch underwrote five corporate convertible zeros under the trade name LYONS, standing for Liquid Yield Option Notes. One issue was from Waste Management, the Illinois-based international disposer of toxic materials. At issue, Waste Management's LYONS sold for $287.50, carried an A rating, and matured in 20 years at par of $1,000. Its LYONS yielded 8.36 percent to maturity and carried a conversion ratio of 4.36 shares of Waste Management stock, then priced at $60.50 per share.

Our first task is to analyze the zero as a bond. We note that its yield is slightly below that available from CATS and TIGRs of 20-year maturity, but we would expect that to be the case because the corporate convertible zero offers the potential for appreciation from the underlying stock. The sacrifice in yield is the economic cost for the conversion feature, so let's look at this bond with reference to its stock.

As noted, the conversion ratio is 4.36 shares. With the bond selling at $287.50, the stock price at conversion is $65.94 (purchase price divided by conversion ratio).

With the common stock of Waste Management selling at $60.50 per share when we bought the convertible corporate zero, we note that we're paying a premium of $5.44 per share for the 4.36 shares of stock we're entitled to if we convert the bond. Therefore, the common stock of Waste Management must approach $66 before it's advantageous to convert the zero to stock.

Even though this may seem to be a disadvantage, we at least know that we're guaranteed ownership of the common stock at a fixed price. Therefore, if Waste Management common stock ever exceeds $66 per share, we have the option of "buying" below market price simply by exercising the conversion privilege. The disadvantage then becomes an advantage—and a source of future gain from the zero. (By the way, to exercise conversion privileges you follow the directions on the bond certificate. Those directions will probably tell you to notify the appropriate official of the corporation, usually the corporate secretary, and/or the corporation's transfer agent, usually a major bank.)

To estimate that potential for gain, we look at the conversion value (the conversion ratio times current market price of the underlying stock). We multiply 4.36 times the current market price of $60.50 for the stock and derive $263.78. In other words, examining the zero as a stock-equivalent, it's worth $263.78.

Again, there wouldn't seem much reason to buy the LYONS instead of buying the stock outright. If we entered the market and bought 4.36 shares of Waste Management stock (actually, you can't buy fractional shares), we'd only pay $263.78. When we buy the zero that's convertible into 4.36 shares, we pay $287.50. Why pay the extra money? Because the zero appreciated with the underlying stock *and* it retains its value as a zero.

Let's say the common stock of Waste Management appreciates to $70 per share. The 4.36 shares we're entitled to as owners of the zero would be worth $305.20. Therefore, the price of the zero would appreciate to $305.20 because the convertible represents a claim on 4.36 shares of stock. The convertible corporate zero will always be worth at least its value on conversion into stock.

However, remember that this zero is also a bond. It will mature to $1,000 regardless of the price of the underlying stock. To pick an extreme illustration, say the price of Waste Management stock falls to $1 per share at the end of 20 years, when the zero matures. If you'd bought 4.36 shares of stock, you'd have an investment worth $4.36. The zero would be worth $1,000. In fact, in order to produce the $1,000 that the zero will produce at maturity, the 4.36 shares of stock would have to appreciate to $229.36 apiece.

That's not likely to happen. But even if it does—even if the price of Waste Management stock goes to $1,000 per share— your zero is still convertible into 4.36 shares. The zero will appreciate in price right alongside the 4.36 shares it's convertible into. Moreover, don't forget that the zero will produce capital gains when interest rates fall regardless of what happens to the stock price. Whether the zero is worth more as a bond or as a stock-equivalent is of little concern to the owner of the zero because it combines the advantages of stock ownership and zero ownership.

DISADVANTAGES

Every investment has disadvantages, and so do corporate zeros.

For one thing, there are very few of them in existence as of 1986, although perhaps their numbers will increase, because these investments are attractive to issuers as well as to buyers. Also, of the five corporate convertible zeros presently outstanding, all are 20-year bonds. You don't have a choice of maturities.

Corporate convertible zeros are potentially more volatile than other zeros. First, they're subject to the same market fluctuations as other zeros when interest rates change, producing capital losses when rates fall. This is a particular disadvantage with corporate zeros because all of them are at present long-term zeros. Second, corporate zeros are backed only by the profitability of the issuer, so their prices will fluctuate with the fortunes of the issuing corporations in addition to fluctuating with the changes in interest rates. Also, if the corporation defaults on its debt, you have only the consolation of being in line to claim the assets of the issuer. There is no full faith and credit backing by Uncle Sam.

Unless you buy them for an IRA or Keogh, they generate current tax liability on phantom interest, as do most zeros held outside tax-deferred accounts.

Finally, corporate convertible zeros are new and untested investments, so issues such as call protection and other matters important to investors in zeros have no track record.

INVESTMENT APPEAL

Just as municipal zeros appeal to investors who like the interest accretion now and current income later, corporate convertible zeros appeal to investors who like to couple the growth possibilities of an equity-equivalent with the advantages of zeros. Such investors are usually long term in their orientation, although, of course, corporate convertible zeros can be played for aggressive gains like any other long-running zero, whether corporate, municipal, or derivative.

SUMMARY

However you add it up, convertible zeros extend the usefulness and profitability of zero coupon investments generally. By combining the capital accumulation feature that zeros are best known for with the extra advantage of current income, convertible zeros offer an attractive inducement to consider further the advantages that this singular investment medium provides. Add to the income-convertibility of municipal convertibles and of EE Savings Bonds the capital growth possibilities of corporate convertibles, and you can assemble a considerable number of advantages in a growing portfolio of zero coupon investments.

6

Indirect Investment in Zero Coupon Funds

Advantageous as zeros are, you might lack the time or inclination or capital to purchase them directly—that is, to phone up brokers and place an order for your account. What's more, if you do prefer to invest directly in zeros, you may not always have the capital to invest when attractive issues are released, or maybe when you have the money to invest there isn't a zero that appeals to you available. In short, when the market is ready maybe you're not, and when you're ready maybe the market isn't. One resolution to this dilemma is to invest indirectly in zeros by subscribing to zero coupon bond funds.

Like customary mutual funds, zero funds assemble money from many investors and buy zeros for all subscribers in the fund. You own shares in the fund, or to express the situation more conveniently than accurately, you own stock in bonds.

ZERO COUPON BOND FUNDS

The zero fund most attractive to zero coupon investors is a "target fund," which is slightly different from a customary mutual fund. Conventional bond funds operate indefinitely, constantly buying and trading bonds in their portfolios, adding and deleting securities according to market conditions. Conventional bond funds have a "weighted average maturity," meaning that they might hold bonds maturing from this year to many years from now. The average maturity is the arithmetic mean maturity of all bonds in the fund, and it is "weighted" to reflect the emphasis on a particular year of maturity in the fund.

Zero target funds do not operate indefinitely, nor do they have average maturities. Fund managers hold bonds maturing in an identified year, and they offer several discreet portfolios within the overall fund. When bonds in a particular portfolio year mature, that portfolio terminates, sends distributions to share owners, and that's that. Zero target fund portfolios are identified by year of maturity. For instance, say a target fund has five portfolios—1990, 1995, 2000, 2005, and 2010. You invest in each portfolio as a separate investment, and every bond in each portfolio matures during the indicated year.

ADVANTAGES OF ZERO TARGET FUNDS

Zero target funds are advantageous for several reasons. They offer all the advantages of conventional mutual funds: Professional managers select bonds, maintain paperwork, send you account records, redeem shares if you sell, offer switch privileges among funds, and—very important—permit you to make additional investments in the fund after you've opened the account. Portfolios in zero target funds don't fluctuate indefinitely in value, as conventional bond funds do. Because bonds mature in an identified year, each portfolio within the fund has a terminal value, and as that year approaches, the net asset value of your investment stabilizes. And most important for investors in zeros, you can select a zero target fund portfolio as you would select a single bond.

Let's say you're interested in intermediate-term zeros. You can enroll in a zero target fund and choose the portfolio of zeros maturing in 1995. You can also make subsequent contributions. In 1995 the fund closes, and you can reevaluate your needs. You can reinvest in a portfolio with a later maturity or cash your holdings. Most zero target funds invest only in zeros derived from Treasury securities, so your money is safe against default. Perhaps someday zero target funds will offer corporate zeros, further expanding the choices open to you.

As with most mutual funds, your purchase price is the fund's net asset value (market value of the fund's securities divided by the number of shares). Most zero funds have no sales charge, but some have yearly account fees. The minimum initial investment for most zero funds is $1,000 (around $250 to $500 for Individual Retirement Accounts), and the minimum for subsequent investments is usually $100. Low minimums for subsequent investment let you take advantage of any investor's most formidable investment ally—dollar cost averaging.

DOLLAR COST AVERAGING

Dollar cost averaging is a simple procedure that requires investing a fixed amount at a fixed interval in a zero fund portfolio. To illustrate dollar cost averaging, let's assume you buy shares of a zero fund portfolio in amounts of $100 each month. Six months from now, your purchase record might look like this:

Month	Net Asset Value	Shares Purchased	Portfolio Value
January	$10 per share	10	$100
February	$ 8	12.5	$180
March	$ 9	11.111	$302.50
April	$10	10	$436.11
May	$11	9.091	$579.72
June	$12	8.333	$732.42

You ended the period with a portfolio value of $732.42 (61.035 total shares times $12 per share on the closing date) on an investment of $600. You achieved that gain because dollar cost averaging buys more shares when net asset values are lower and fewer shares when they're higher.

Dollar cost averaging is especially useful for zero funds because funds permit you to buy fractional shares, whereas you can't buy part of a zero if you purchase it directly. Once you've decided to invest in zero funds, dollar cost averaging eliminates timing decisions, because you automatically profit from buying more shares of a zero fund when its net asset value is depressed. In addition, you—not the market—establish how much you invest per period through dollar cost averaging.

However, dollar cost averaging doesn't assure continual gains, because net asset values fluctuate. Note February. Two months into dollar costing, you'd placed $200 into a zero fund valued at $180 (22.5 shares at $8 per share). Had you redeemed the shares, you'd have lost 10 percent of your investment. By continuing to dollar cost, you bought more shares at net asset values of $8 and $9 and benefited when net asset values improved because you were holding more shares.

With conventional bond funds, share prices can fall indefinitely, but a target fund has a terminal maturity. Over time, the average net asset value of shares purchased through dollar cost averaging will be less than their price when the fund matures.

(Dollar costing can be effective for direct purchases of zeros, because they're inexpensive and usually fluctuate enough to be acquired advantageously through dollar costing, although commissions erode gains. If you want to follow this strategy as a direct investor, your best bet is to dollar cost long-term zeros, for they produce the greater price fluctuations necessary for maximum advantage from dollar costing. Unless you are dollar costing long-term zeros monthly or quarterly and are prepared to hold them several years, dollar costing zeros won't produce returns as advantageously as it will with zero funds.)

Zero funds also produce taxation on phantom interest, but again, many investors don't find that a disadvantage. Reinvested interest on *all* bond funds (excluding municipal bond funds) is federally taxable, and essentially interest *is* continually reinvested with your zero fund. Also, remember what we said earlier: Too often, we don't let coupon interest compound; we spend it right away, and we end up merely getting par value back. We pay taxes on that dissipated interest, too. So there may be a real advantage to zero funds despite taxation on phantom income, and their situation isn't any worse than the norm. If you dislike paying taxes on interest you haven't actually frittered away, you have two alternatives.

First, invest your IRA or Keogh in zero funds to compound untaxed, or use zero funds for Uniform Gifts to Minors Accounts (UGMAs), for which taxable phantom interest is negligible. If you buy zeros for your IRA, dollar cost averaging is a disciplined way to set aside your maximum yearly contribution, and dollar costing UGMAs is a convenient way to attend to your children's future.

Second, invest in zero funds that hold federally tax-exempt zero coupon municipal securities.

FEDERALLY TAX-EXEMPT ZERO FUNDS

Familiar to most investors, the two best-known types of indirect investments offering municipal securities are the municipal bond fund and the municipal securities trust. For people seeking indirect investment in municipal zeros, however, these two familiar vehicles aren't useful. Municipal bond mutual funds don't invest in zeros, and rarely will municipal securities trusts mix zeros with coupon-paying municipals. But investing in a portfolio of zero coupon municipals is possible through an investment vehicle similar to a mutual fund and to a municiple securities trust. It's called a tax-exempt securities trust.

A tax-exempt securities trust is similar to a municipal bond mutual fund in that it takes money from many investors and purchases a portfolio of municipal bonds in which each investor owns a part (as we noted, though, municipal bond funds buy only coupon-paying municipals). That, too, is the principal behind the conventional municipal securities trust, which also invests in coupon-paying municipal bonds.

Like the municipal securities trust, the tax exempt securities trust is usually an unmanaged portfolio. Whereas mutual bond fund managers will constantly add and delete securities from their fund's holdings, managers of municipal securities trusts and tax exempt securities trusts operate a fixed portfolio. Unless market conditions change drastically or unless an issue within the trust deteriorates substantially in its creditworthiness, managers of a municipal trust won't alter the composition of the trust's holdings.

Managers of tax exempt securities trusts have discovered the popularity of zero coupon municipals and have also discovered that the two best-known forms of indirect municipal investment haven't moved to capitalize on zeros' popularity. Accordingly, they have created portfolios of municipal zeros and offered them to investors who don't want to buy municipals directly.

With zero coupon municipals, accreted interest is federally untaxable, and tax-exempt securities trusts holding municipal zeros also escape federal tax. State tax may or may not apply in your state, and infrequent capital gains will be fully taxed. Tax-exempt securities trusts pass on the tax advantages and the investment advantages of the trust to you. In addition, they offer the advantages associated with professional management and recordkeeping services.

The chief disadvantage with tax-exempt securities trusts is that they aren't target funds, so they don't have precise maturities and interest rates. The trust will terminate at some distant point, but not all of its zeros mature in the same year. Tax-exempt securities trusts hold several series of maturities, and the whole portfolio won't mature at once. We've cited maturity as an important criterion in selecting municipal zeros. Thus, from the point of view of known maturity, tax exempt securities trusts are slightly disadvantaged.

As an investor in a tax-exempt securities trust, you buy "units" in a comprehensive portfolio, and you'll be quoted a yield to average maturity. The minimum purchase is usually 5 or 10 units, requiring an initial investment of $5,000 to $10,000. Most tax-exempt securities trusts are diversified with municipal zeros from many states, adding safety should any issue default.

Dollar cost averaging usually isn't possible with tax-exempt securities trusts. They don't usually permit subsequent investments because the portfolio is fixed. Some do, but, unlike target funds, trusts generally won't accept subsequent deposits and buy more bonds. You can buy additional units from sponsoring brokerages if they have any in inventory. Otherwise, you can't buy additional units unless another investor will sell them. At worst, you'll have to wait for another series of the trust, and you'll likely not have a long wait. Consult the Appendix for issuers of tax-exempt securities trusts.

ZERO COUPON FUNDS COUPLED WITH COMMODITIES

Late in 1985, Shearson Lehman Brothers, a unit of American Express, designed a zero fund that mates the capital assurance features of zeros with aggressive investments in commodities and futures, perhaps the most speculative of all investment vehicles. This selected type of zero fund offers the chance for aggressive gains through commodities trading *and* assures investors who hold the fund until maturity that they'll at least get their original investment back. Consequently, it provides a form of aggressive investment that virtually eliminates the prospect of total capital loss so prevalent with outright commodities trading or investment in commodity funds.

The fund, called Shearson Lehman Futures 1000 Fund, requires you to invest at least $5,000 for five years ($2,000 for an IRA). The managers take about half of your investment and place the money in Treasury derivative zeros or STRIPS. With the present levels of interest rates, this half of the investment will grow to equal the amount of your original investment in five years.

The other half of your investment is placed into futures and commodities contracts—currencies and financial futures, metals, agricultural futures, energy futures, stock indexes, and whatever else looks promising—in an attempt to produce extraordinary gains.

Apart from assurance that you won't go absolutely broke—in fact, you should receive about all of your original capital back if you stay in the fund for five years—you have diversification within a portfolio of commodities and futures investments and the advantage of professional managers investing on your behalf in these intensely volatile markets.

The Shearson Lehman 1000 Futures Fund, and the many competitors from other institutions that surely will follow, offers an excellent way to participate in the capital accumulation features of zeros and the exponential gains of futures trading. In addition, other advantages of the fund include no management fee (an incentive fee will apply on a percentage of profits, and the Shearson broker from whom you bought the fund will receive $40 per each $1,000 you invest), restriction of margin responsibility to the fund managers, and interest paid on cash balances.

If necessary, you can redeem your units in the fund upon appropriate written notification, although you aren't assured of preserving capital or securing an investment gain if you redeem your units before five years.

If you're interested in the aggressive possibilities from this type of novel investment, you'll have to meet suitability requirements. You'll have to show net worth of at least $75,000 excluding home and personal possessions or a minimum net worth of $30,000 plus an annual income of at least $30,000. Suitability standards may be higher in some states.

Shearson's innovative approach in creating an extremely aggressive investment with minimal downside risk shows the exceptional range of possibilities that zeros afford. Even if you aren't interested in this type of zero coupon innovation, you should at least appreciate by now how incredibly versatile zeros are and how innovative you can be in using them in many financial circumstances.

UNIT INVESTMENT TRUSTS FOR CAPITAL GROWTH

Even if the aggressive intentions of an investment that mates zeros with commodities trading is too speculative for your tastes, nearly every investor needs to be concerned with long-term capital growth, and now there's a vehicle that mates zeros with selected growth stocks to provide stability of principal plus capital gains. This new zero "fund" is a unit investment trust called Paine Webber Pathfinders Trust offered by Paine, Webber Inc., a national investment house.

The trust works much like the Shearson Futures 1000 program, except that Paine Webber managers select promising growth stocks instead of commodities to complement the portfolio of derivative zeros. We'll examine in Part Two how to structure a personal portfolio of zeros in concert with growth equities, and we'll see there that combining zeros with growth stocks can maximize the advantages of capital growth with the guaranteed accumulations of zeros. The advantage to the Paine Webber program is that professional money managers pick the promising stocks and maintain account paperwork.

In a nutshell, the Pathfinders Trust works as follows, taking as our example Series 3 of the trust, which was offered in early 1986.

When initially offered to the public, Pathfinders was priced at $1 per unit, with the minimum initial investment being $1,000 ($250 for Individual Retirement Accounts). Slightly more than half of the investment was placed in zero coupon Treasury derivatives maturing in 1994, and the remaining portion was invested in common stocks that the portfolio managers believed to have above-average potential for capital growth by 1994.

At the prices and interest rates available in early 1986, the zero coupon component of the trust will pay back the initial investment upon maturity in 1994. Therefore, even if the stock component of the portfolio returns no gains—an unlikely possibility—investors are assured of receiving their initial investment back if they hold the trust to maturity. Meanwhile, the dividends and price appreciation from the stock component provide capital growth.

As a fixed portfolio the trust doesn't engage in active trading, as would be the case with a conventional fund, so transaction fees are negligible. Intermittent costs of managing the fund are paid from dividends collected from the stocks in the portfolio. The remaining dividends are paid semiannually to investors in the trust, and long-term capital gains are paid annually.

The entire series of the trust terminates within 15 days after maturity of the zeros. Approximately 30 days before the zeros mature, the trust will begin to sell the stocks in its portfolio, and all terminal proceeds will be distributed to investors in the trust.

Paine Webber intends to make a secondary market for unit-holders who want to sell their participations before the trust matures, and Paine Webber also offers limited exchange and transfer privileges with other investments offered through the company. Held outside IRAs, the trust will produce phantom taxable interest from the zeros in the portfolio, but for reasons we've noted often, that doesn't have to be a major deterrent. What should probably be a bit more disconcerting is the trust's intention to hold a fixed portfolio of stocks for eight years. Although the trust's managers can sell their stocks under specified conditions, most investors may question the desirability of investing in an essentially fixed equity portfolio.

These potential disadvantages aside, Pathfinders Trust and the similar vehicles that competitors will surely offer illustrate how you can profit from indirect ownership in zeros while striving for capital gains in a single investment. In addition, they also point out the growing versatility of zeros, particularly when combined with other kinds of investments in a program of indirect ownership.

MONEY MARKET FUNDS

If you're a contemporary American investor, you're probably already investing in a zero coupon fund without knowing it. In Chapter 3 where we covered original issue zeros, we mentioned several types of investments—specifically, T-bills, commercial paper, repurchase agreements, and international letters of credit—that generally are too high-priced for most individual investors. These vehicles are high-quality, short-term obligations maturing in a few days to less than a year, and they're generally offered by major financial institutions and corporations. Nearly all are zero coupon investments that pay interest as the difference between purchase price and maturity value ("par" isn't exactly the right term to describe the terminal value of these investments).

Even if these investments are too rich for your wallet, they're purchased in sizable quantity by managers of money market funds, and they're available to you as an indirect investor who subscribes to the fund. For as little as $1,000 and often less, you can become part owner of a portfolio of these investments and add the advantages of very short-term zeros to your holdings.

The chief advantage to money funds is their constant net asset value. Because the zeros in a money fund mature so quickly, the net asset value of your fund remains at a constant $1. There's no capital fluctuation, a key disadvantage of zeros for some investors. Therefore, they're excellent savings vehicles and are also useful as a temporary parking lot for cash awaiting investment elsewhere. In addition, money funds pay market-level returns that have varied between 5 and 20 percent in the recent past.

Moreover, money market funds offer instant liquidity without commissions. Most funds feature checking privileges that permit you to cash your holdings in a familiar manner, and what few money funds don't offer checking will have telephone redemption features. There are three types of money funds. The first invests exclusively in T-bills and other government paper for maximum security. The second invests in T-bills and corporate paper for maximum returns. The third invests in short-term municipal paper for federally untaxed returns, a major advantage for highly taxed investors.

If you're one of few investors who isn't conversant with money market funds, consult *Starting Small, Investing Smart* (Homewood, Ill.: Dow Jones-Irwin, 1984), your author's first book, for particulars. You can subscribe to a money market fund through any mutual fund family, a bank or S&L, and virtually any full-service or discount brokerage. Although not commonly thought of as a zero coupon fund, that's exactly what money market funds are. You're probably already investing in a money fund, and that should give you greater confidence to invest in other types of zero coupon funds.

SUMMARY

Zero coupon funds offer many of the advantages of direct investment in zeros. They can serve a range of portfolio strategies and time horizons while minimizing your investment. Zero funds make capital markets more accessible for less-capitalized investors, and they definitely deserve consideration as part of your total holdings of zeros.

Managing Zero Coupon Investments

7

Zeros and the Savings Component
of the Portfolio

By definition, a smart saver is a smart investor, and smart investors would no more expand their portfolios without assuring their savings are in order than an engineer would attempt to build a pyramid by starting at the tip. Most financial counselors would advise you to hold 10 to 25 percent of your yearly net income in savings, depending upon your age, employment situation, and personal circumstances.

When we speak of "savings," we're really talking about a specific kind of investment—one that earns market-level returns, fluctuates minimally in value, and is easily converted to cash. In addition, minimizing commissions is very important in choosing savings-type investments, because their market-level returns, although gratifying, don't generate the exponential gains that offset commissions. With returns, capital stability, liquidity, and minimum commissions as our goals, you'd probably agree that most zeros aren't suited for the savings component.

Zero coupon CDs are highly stable, but they often bear interest penalties if redeemed before maturity, so they don't provide ready liquidity. EE Savings Bonds are suited for what you might call long-term savings because they're invulnerable to market fluctuations, but they're illiquid before six months'

ownership and don't pay market-level interest in their early
years. Long-term corporate and derivative zeros fluctuate too
much in price, and commissions usually apply to purchase and
sale. Zero bond funds are less advantaged for the savings component as we define it, although they can serve some types of
savings situations. But by the time you've read this far you've
learned not to rule out zeros for any portfolio purpose.

U.S. TREASURY BILLS

One zero coupon investment that's right for the savings component of the portfolio is the U.S. Treasury bill, assuming you can
come up with the $10,000 minimum required to buy one. As
we noted in Chapter 3, T-bills are short-term obligations of the
U.S. Treasury that sell at discounts below par and mature in 13,
26, and 52 weeks. Brief maturities assure relative capital stability, and, as the next best thing to cash, they're easily sold if you
need the money. Their returns are the measure of market-level
returns, so there's no problem in earning what the market will
pay.

You can buy T-bills from any full-service brokerage firm and
most discount brokerages, and commissions will range from $30
to $100. Most banks and S&Ls will buy bills for you, although
their fees often exceed commissions from brokers. If you have a
substantial account or a longstanding relationship with a depos-
itory institution, however, it may charge minimal fees to maintain your good will.

A commission-free but slightly inconvenient way to buy T-
bills is to purchase them directly from a Federal Reserve Bank
or branch through a process called noncompetitive tender.

Every week, the Treasury refinances billions of dollars worth
of existing T-bills and floats new ones. Major national and
international financial institutions, depositories of all sizes, and
well-capitalized private investors submit "competitive tenders"
for these securities. That is, they study markets and interest rate
trends and attempt to achieve the highest returns by specifying a
price at which they'll purchase T-bills during weekly auctions.
The lower the price for a given maturity, the higher the yield.
These institutions and investors, therefore, attempt to secure
the highest yield by specifying a specific purchase price through
a competitive tender.

By submitting a noncompetitive tender, however, you in-form the Federal Reserve, as agent for the Treasury, that you'll pay the average price and accept the average yield at which the T-bills are auctioned. Although you may receive a decimal lower interest than big-money buyers who study T-bill markets full-time, you're almost assured of receiving a T-bill because the Federal Reserve fills noncompetitive tenders first. Of course, you can submit a competitive tender just like the major buyers, but if your offer isn't accepted, you don't get your bills.

Call or write the nearest Federal Reserve Bank or branch, and representatives will mail you complete information about buying T-bills, including preprinted forms for executing the transaction. However, the forms aren't necessary. You can write the Federal Reserve a letter indicating you want to submit a noncompetitive tender. Specify the date of the auction, and indicate the maturity you're interested in.

Mail or hand deliver your letter to the Fed along with a cashier's check for at least $10,000, the minimum purchase price for one bill. T-bills are also sold in increments of $5,000 beyond the minimum, so you can purchase bills for $10,000, $15,000, and so on.

You pay the full par value when you submit your offer. When your offer is accepted, the Federal Reserve will mail you a check for the difference between par value and average purchase price. If, for example, 13-week bills sell for an average of $9,500, you'll receive a check for $500. The check is a return of principal and is untaxed.

Your T-bill will be registered in book entry form on computer tape. You'll receive a confirmation notice indicating the registration number of your bill and its maturity.

The most convenient way to manage your T-bills is to roll them over at the end of each maturity period, automatically buying a new bill of the same maturity when the old one matures. If you intend to roll bills over, so indicate when you buy bills initially. The Federal Reserve, broker, or banking agent will execute your intention as another noncompetitive tender when the bill matures. You pay no commissions or fees on T-bill rollovers.

When you purchase the subsequent bill, you will once again receive a check for the difference between par value and average purchase price. However, in this case, the check represents interest paid on the preceding T-bill.

The check may be more or less than actual interest received, depending upon the average price of T-bills at the second auction. For example, for the first noncompetitive tender you paid $9,500 for a $10,000 T-bill, and you got back $500, which was a return of capital. When that bill matures, you'll receive $10,000. However, perhaps at the second auction T-bills sell for $9,600—$100 more. When you roll the first T-bill over and use it to buy a second bill, you'll receive a check for $400, but you'll still have received $500 in federally taxable interest. Like any other borrower to whom you loan money, the Treasury will apprise you of interest earned, which makes your recordkeeping easier.

Of course, you don't have to buy T-bills when they're originally issued. You can buy them anytime in the open market through brokers and depositaries. In this case, the market will establish the price, not the average price that prevailed when you submitted a noncompetitive tender.

If you hold a T-bill until maturity, your payment will be interest (subject to federal tax but exempt from state and local taxes). But if you sell your T-bill prior to maturity, the difference between your purchase price and sale price will be a capital gain or loss. Interest isn't taxable until the bill matures. Capital gains are taxed and capital losses declared for the year in which you sold the bill.

OTHER ZEROS FOR SAVINGS

Of course, any zero with a short-term maturity offers liquidity and relative capital stability. Zeros maturing in two years or less will be less volatile than their long-running counterparts, so they have the relative stability needed for savings, and public markets make them liquid, although their usefulness as savings will be diminished by commissions.

Near-term corporate or derivative zeros are possible choices for the savings component, although near-term zeros from funds might be a better choice. The initial investment will be lower than for direct purchase of zeros—certainly lower than for direct purchase of T-bills—and low minimums for subsequent investment are attractive for savers. Commissions are likely to be lower, also.

If direct purchase of zeros or indirect investment in zero funds proves advantageous, following these guidelines will help make the most of zeros in the savings component.

First, select near-term zeros maturing in the same year. That way, if you do need to sell your zeros for an emergency, you needn't expend commissions selling different series of zeros. If you're investing in a zero fund, pick the nearest-term portfolio and contribute to it regularly. If you have to redeem shares, you'll have your money in one place and won't have to execute multiple redemptions.

Second, try to buy and hold your savings zeros with a brokerage firm that maintains its own market. If you must sell before the bonds mature, perhaps you'll escape with lesser commissions than if you bought your zeros in public markets.

Third, if you aren't forced to sell or redeem zeros for an emergency and are able to hold them until maturity, reinvest their proceeds immediately in another series of zeros or in another portfolio of the zero fund.

By following these steps, you can use zeros other than T-bills in the savings component of the portfolio, although the former are, for reasons we've seen, preferable for savings.

MONEY MARKET FUNDS

Before deciding upon directly purchased zeros or zero funds as savings vehicles, though, compare the rates and advantages of more conventional savings instruments like money market funds. In reality a special type of zero coupon fund, money market funds offer market-level returns, liquidity by check, no capital fluctuation, and no commissions or fees. That combination fits perfectly with the needs of the savings component. Also, they're a form of indirect investment in zeros, for most money funds hold T-bills, repurchase agreements, and other types of original-issue, short-term zeros. With their low minimums for initial and subsequent investment, money market funds are the ideal vehicle for serving the savings component of the portfolio. They're the perfect way to invest in zeros for savings.

SUMMARY

What we've seen in this chapter—and will see in following chapters—is that zero coupon investments can serve the portfolio in ways most people don't think possible. In this case, we've looked at T-bills as the original issue zero most favorable to savings, but we've seen that other types of zeros, though less useful, can still serve the savings component of the portfolio. Finally, we noted that money market funds, a special type of zero coupon fund, are the preferred savings investment. What we'll see in subsequent chapters is that zeros serve other components of the portfolio equally well.

8

Zeros and the Current Income Component of the Portfolio

The most frequent criticism of zero coupon investments is that they are useless to investors who need or prefer current income investments. Such investors are the retired, who need dividends and interest to supplement pensions, social security, and retirement plans, and investors of all ages who prefer current income investments because they can reinvest interest and dividends for compound growth.

We've seen that these criticisms don't hold for two types of zero coupon investments—the convertible municipal bond and EE Savings Bonds convertible into coupon-paying HH bonds. As we're about to learn, even though other types of zeros don't pay interest until maturity, zeros can be arranged to produce current income by scheduling maturities carefully. But taking first things first, let's begin our discussion of zeros and the current income component by looking at convertible issues.

CONVERTIBLE MUNICIPAL ZEROS

As we noted in Chapter 5, convertible municipal zeros grow as ordinary zero coupon bonds for a certain period and then automatically become conventional, coupon-paying bonds. Because of their predictable growth and predictable period of income payments, convertible zeros are exceedingly useful, perhaps even preferable, alternatives to annuities in retirement planning. Their conversion to income investments is specified in the bond covenant, and you need take no action to begin receiving income from these instruments. You do, however, have to plan for periods of capital accumulation and income when purchasing them.

At present, most issues of convertible municipal zeros hold their capital accumulation phase for 10 to 12 years before converting to income investments. Obviously, the easiest way to manage them is to buy them around a decade before you think you'll need their income. If you plan to retire at age 65, go shopping for convertible zeros in your mid-to-late fifties. Their current income phase should conveniently coincide with the beginning of your retirement.

Bear in mind, though, that you may have different needs for income at different periods of retirement. If, for example, you purchased an annuity, perhaps its income stream coupled with social security and pension will be sufficient for your early retirement years. In this case, perhaps you need current income from convertibles at a later stage of your retirement, in which case you can postpone buying convertibles in your preretirement years.

On the other hand, perhaps you'll need greater income early in your retirement—say, if you have children finishing college during your midsixties or if you're expecting some other temporary drain on your finances. In this case, you'll want to arrange maximum payments earlier in your retirement.

Whatever your particular situation, you need to plan your convertible municipal zeros for payments that suit your needs. That means you must assess your sources of retirement income—IRAs, social security, personal investments, pensions, and rental payments—and determine how your convertibles can best fit with your other sources of income.

EE AND HH SAVINGS BONDS

The same holds true for converting EE Savings Bonds into coupon-paying HH bonds. In Chapter 5, we outlined how this procedure can work to your advantage. You exchange your zero coupon EE bonds, retaining their federal tax deferral if you wish, for HH bonds by mailing them to the Department of the Treasury or a Federal Reserve Bank or branch. When doing so, however, you must decide the frequency of income you need from HH bonds, because, unlike other Treasury bonds, the date of semiannual interest payments from HH bonds is established on the date of conversion.

If you bought a publicly traded Treasury bond, it would pay interest semiannually on a date established when the bond was issued, regardless of when you purchased it. So if you bought a bond maturing in May of any year, it will pay interest in May and November every year until it matures. Buy a bond maturing in June, and it will pay semiannual interest in June and December. And so on throughout the calendar.

However, when you convert EE bonds to HH bonds, you'll begin receiving coupon interest payments (7.5 percent of par value) six months from the date of conversion. Your date of conversion establishes the schedule of semiannual interest. If you ship in all your matured EE bonds at once, you'll receive income only twice yearly. But if you convert your EE bonds serially—convert some in January, some in February, and so on—you'll establish a more frequent payment schedule for your HH bonds. Bonds converted in January will pay interest in July and January; in February, August and February; in March, September and March—and so on.

As always, you must assess your needs for current income and arrange conversion of your EE Savings Bonds accordingly. However, you can make the most of scheduling income from zeros by carefully arranging maturities in other ways, and in this case you can take full advantage of the range of zeros available. The example we're about to examine is an instance of an investor contriving current income by investing a lump-sum distribution from an employer. The same principle holds for managing any distribution, be it a matured IRA, a portfolio of other zeros, a life insurance or estate settlement, or a single payment from an annuity.

ARRANGING CURRENT INCOME BY SERIALIZED MATURITIES

In arranging zeros to provide current income, we rely upon the most convenient characteristic of zeros: their single payment upon maturity. It doesn't matter if the zero is a TIGR, a CD, a municipal or corporate zero, or a zero coupon fund. You can serialize zeros to receive a predictable payment. In this case, we're taking the example of a lump-sum distribution from an employer because it's a frequent occurrence with established rules and permits rolling over into a tax-deferred account. After we've established the pattern in the example, we'll see how it can be extended to other situations.

Let's say that you retire at age 59 and receive a single distribution from your employee investment plan. At present, tax law permits you to, among other alternatives, place those proceeds into an IRA Rollover Account. In the rollover, as with standard IRAs, tax is deferred until you accept a payment as fully taxable current income. In this case, you can take the lump-sum distribution and purchase zeros of serialized yearly maturities. As each zero matures, you can accept the proceeds and use them for current income (or reinvestment). We'll use a 10-year term for convenience, although you can arrange any schedule that fits your circumstances, and we'll assume the lump-sum distribution is $100,000.

Let's say that you decide to invest 10 increments of approximately $10,000, although, of course, you can arrange any apportionment that you prefer. Your schedule might resemble this, but remember that prices change daily and these are only approximations:

Age	Year	Cost per Zero	Total Outlay	Total Accumulations
60	1	$870	$ 9,570	$ 11,000
61	2	800	9,600	12,000
62	3	735	9,555	13,000
63	4	600	9,600	16,000
64	5	550	9,900	18,000
65	6	490	9,800	20,000
66	7	400	10,000	25,000
67	8	370	9,990	27,000
68	9	350	9,800	28,000
69	10	333	9,990	30,000
		Investment totals	97,805	200,000

Although we've not considered commissions, we can see that you not only receive yearly income of the amount indicated at the right but also turn $100,000 into $200,000 without exaggerated market maneuvering. This particular example arranges greater income in later years, but with a little shuffling of money up front you can twist the income schedule any way you prefer. One disadvantage with this arrangement is that you receive income only once yearly when the zeros mature. However, remember that this schedule supplements any other income you may receive.

A schedule of this type lets you see when your investments are maturing and aids your planning. You can prepare it by hand or keep it on file and currently updated in a home computer. For your further convenience, we have a worksheet in the Appendix that you can photocopy for use throughout portfolio planning. You'll also see something resembling this chart in our chapter on zero coupon investments and the lump-sum component of the portfolio. It's very useful in helping you maximize the planning certainty of zeros, whether you're planning for income or arranging any other aspect of your portfolio.

The particular advantage of zeros in the current income component of the portfolio is that you can select a variety of zero coupon investments. If there isn't a CAT or TIGR maturing in a given year, select a corporate zero, a zero CD, or a zero bond fund with a compatible maturity. Now that you know the types of zeros available, you can choose among them for your convenience and profit, selecting maturities you need from the range of zeros available.

This example has been of a tax-deferred IRA Rollover, but you can use this schedule for any of your zero coupon investments, including savings bonds, municipals, and funds, even though different tax considerations may apply. (You would not, for example, want zero coupon municipal bonds in a tax-deferred IRA or IRA Rollover Account.)

Just to illustrate how to fit zeros into the current income component, let's review the portfolio of a real investor, a 62-year-old widow who's just received a life insurance settlement from her late husband's insurance company. In this investor's case, current income from part-time work and other investments is more than adequate for current needs. She plans to work part-time for three years, and then she would like to live off the proceeds of investing her insurance settlement.

Although not a sophisticated investor, she readily grasps the basics and advantages of zero coupon investments, and her financial adviser has worked out the following arrangement for her. Because we're interested in examining the diversity of zeros in providing current income and not their accumulations, we'll merely list her investments and not report their dollar value or par values.

Year	Age	Zero Coupon Investment
1989	65	Money market fund
1990	66	Zero coupon target fund with 1990 maturity
1991	67	Zero coupon CD purchased from a brokerage
1992	68	Derivative zero purchased from a brokerage
1993	69	Derivative zero purchased from a brokerage
1994	70	Derivative zero purchased from a brokerage
1995	71	Zero coupon municipal bond
1996	72	Zero coupon municipal bond

With this arrangement, our investor will have an assured source of income for the next decade as a supplement to pension, social security, and investment income. Because taxes are a minimal consideration in this case, the investor and her adviser have agreed simply to pay them as necessary. The two issues of zero coupon municipals are present not for tax considerations but because they happened to be exceptional zeros at the time of purchase. The money market fund is favored for the first year of retirement for three reasons: (1) the adviser could find no attractive zeros with three-year maturities; (2) it serves as a backup savings account; and (3) its immediate liquidity will permit the investor to take a world cruise as a retirement present to herself. As it happens, this investor also has some EE Savings Bonds that will mature in 1989. She may decide what to do with them—cash them or convert them to HH bonds—at her leisure when the time comes.

Obviously, for other types of investors other portfolio decisions would be more appropriate. A highly taxed investor would want a greater weighting of municipal zeros, for instance, or an investor more concerned with capital stability might invest only in the shortest zeros, trusting to self-discipline to reinvest for each additional year. Whatever the need or preference in a current income portfolio, serializing zeros of different maturities can provide it.

MUNICIPAL INVESTMENT TRUSTS

Another option you may want to consider for the income component of your portfolio is a municipal investment trust containing zeros along with current income bonds. We mentioned municipal investment trusts in our discussion of tax exempt securities trusts.

A municipal trust permits you to receive federally untaxed

current income as an indirect owner of a portfolio of municipal bonds. Most trusts give you the option of monthly, quarterly, semiannual, or annual payments. The trust matures as the municipal bonds in its portfolio mature, and your prorated portion of the trust's maturity value is returned to you as a repayment of principal.

Of major benefit to investors in the 30-percent-plus tax bracket, municipal investment trusts have only recently added a zero coupon bond component to their offerings. (The tax-exempt securities trust, remember, has a substantial component of zero municipals.) With the addition of municipal zeros to the trust, you receive federally untaxed capital growth along with federally untaxed current income. Consequently, some municipal trusts are a combination of a current income fund and a tax-exempt securities trust, although, as we've noted, there aren't any straight zero coupon municipal bond funds as yet on the market.

There are many municipal investment trusts on the market, and more are issued all the time, but not all contain a zero coupon component, so you have to check the prospectus carefully if you want a fund with municipal zeros. One of the best-known municipal investment trusts is sponsored by Nuveen and Co., which pioneered the concept that's been adopted by other national financial intermediaries. The Kemper organization, which offers a family of mutual funds and other financial services, also issues municipal investment trusts. Gabriele, Hueglin & Cashman, Inc., the market maker in original issue zero coupon bonds previously mentioned, is an excellent source of municipal investment trusts, coupon-paying municipal bonds, and derivative zeros.

SUMMARY

As we've seen, zero coupon investments can be structured to provide current income, thus overcoming one criticism of zeros. Whether you're buying zeros that convert to current income investments or scheduling maturities to receive current income, you can take charge of your portfolio and use zeros' convenience and predictability to receive the cash you need. With a clear and simple schedule, you can improvise the payments best for you, whether that means income from tax-deferred accounts, savings bonds, municipal zeros, or zero funds.

9

Zeros and the Capital Growth Component of the Portfolio

By "capital growth" we generally mean investments that offer the chance for steady appreciation in price. Strictly speaking, zero coupon investments are not capital growth investments. Let's look first at why they're not, and then we'll look at why it doesn't matter that they're not.

Zero CDs and EE Savings Bonds aside, zeros do appreciate in price, but the source of their appreciation is their approaching maturity and their intense sensitivity to interest rates. Capital growth from stocks, real estate, collectibles, and metals derives from a different source. Nor do zeros provide steady price appreciation. Even though they theoretically increase in price each year, and practically often do so, zeros' intense sensitivity to interest rates often precludes predictable increases in price. As contractual, interest-paying securities, their only actual payments accrue when they mature. Further, capital growth is taxable only when capital gains are taken; zeros generally produce yearly tax liability unless held in tax-deferred accounts (EE Savings Bonds excepted).

However, even though they aren't strictly defined as capital growth investments, zeros are serving functions which conventional growth investments used to serve. Many investors now prefer zeros over conventional growth investments, and others use them to supplement growth securities. Sophisticated investors use zeros in strategies that we'll examine. We've already seen a few reasons why zeros are supplanting stocks and other growth vehicles.

First, they provide predictable accumulations when held to maturity, and other growth investments provide no such guarantee of an ultimate payoff.

Second, zeros don't require intricate analysis, as do stocks, nor do they participate in limited markets, as do collectibles, and they don't suffer the illiquidity and fees of real estate.

Third, throughout their admittedly limited history, zeros have produced real and tax-adjusted returns that have exceeded historical returns from many types of growth investments.

Even though the stock market was 40 months into a bull market in early 1986, historical research shows that the broad market averages produced about 12 percent gains over the two-decade period ending in 1980, and that includes reinvested dividends and excludes capital gains taxation. Certainly, sagacious pickers of stocks earned much higher returns during the period of study, and in rampant bull markets most investors can do better than 12 percent. But when it comes to your everyday investor in everyday markets, 12 percent has been about it for stocks, and that's an average return that works both ways: during some periods the broad indexes of stocks produced substantially smaller, and in some cases negative, returns. In contrast, today's 20-year zero coupon securities are earning at least 10 percent to maturity, and as of 1986 some single-A municipal zeros are yielding close to 10 percent federally untaxed. Any way you look at the norms, zeros rival conventional growth securities on an investment-versus-investment basis.

Zeros certainly aren't going to push customary capital growth investments off the financial pages, because they don't provide the potentially unlimited price appreciation that other growth investments can offer. But on the average, zero coupon securities deserve consideration in the capital growth component of the portfolio. Certainly, the first type of zero that has capital growth uses is the convertible corporate zero.

CONVERTIBLE ZEROS

Convertible zeros from corporations are, at present anyway, few in number, but as we saw in Chapter 5, they offer the twin advantages of other convertible bonds: as bonds, they provide predictable payments upon maturity, and conversion privileges give the potential for capital gains from the underlying stock. Accordingly, these hybrid zeros can serve the growth component in the same way that other convertible corporate bonds do by acting as a proxy for an equity investment. As more corporations recognize the attractiveness of convertible zeros, their numbers should increase, giving investors more issues to use in the growth component of their portfolios. Keep these in mind when considering capital growth investments.

However, you don't have to concentrate on zeros with special features in building the growth component of your investment plan. Derivative and original issue zeros, as well as zero funds, can also serve the growth element of the portfolio.

USING ZEROS IN PLACE OF OTHER GROWTH SECURITIES

If you're investing for steady gains—the definition of capital growth—zeros maturing in around five years provide them while purchase price marches relatively predictably toward par. As a near-term zero or short-term zero fund nears maturity its price approaches par, in effect amortizing phantom interest. (With zeros, this phenomenon is called false appreciation; zeros pay no interim interest, but the market traces "paid" phantom interest through prices as zeros near maturity. Something similar happens with coupon-paying bonds selling below par.) Even though this price increase really isn't capital appreciation, zeros should be worth more each year you hold them, and steady increases are what you want in the capital growth component of the portfolio.

Consequently, some investors avoid standard growth investments in favor of zeros unless alternatives offer exceptional gains. In other words, using zeros to measure opportunity cost revealed that zeros presented the greatest growth, even though it's through amortized interest rather than true capital gains. During markets in which zeros will likely outperform standard growth investments, most investors choose maturities of five years or less. Restraining maturities gives them the chance to reinvest par value if market circumstances change. Further, price growth isn't steady with longer zeros because they're so sensitive to long-term interest rates.

For instance, in 1986 let's say that you bought a zero maturing in 20 years. In 1988, its price may not have appreciated substantially because the slightly decreased term of maturity—18 years instead of 20—won't overcome the influence of long-term interest rates. On the other hand, if you'd bought a zero maturing in, say, 1990, you'd have some movement in price because the bond's close maturity makes it less vulnerable to long-term rates. So if you buy long-term zeros, price gains may lag during early years of ownership, and that doesn't serve the intention of growth.

In addition, sensitivity to interest rates may actually cause sharp declines in prices, and that's absolutely counter to growth. Therefore, when using any zero coupon investment—corporates, municipals, derivatives, funds, CDs—as an alternative to standard growth investments, keep maturities short.

(However, aggressive gains investors prefer the longest maturities for reasons we'll cover in Chapter 10. The longest maturities provide true capital appreciation by coupling amortized phantom interest with declines in interest rates. This, however, is an aggressive gains strategy, not a long-term capital gains strategy, so we'll discuss it in the next chapter.)

In selecting zeros over standard growth investments, remember that you're usually expected to declare phantom interest yearly. Some advisers will insist that taxation on phantom interest should deter you entirely from holding zeros outside IRAs, Keoghs, and low-tax or tax-deferred accounts. We've already seen why such advice should be discounted. Refer yourself or a nay-sayer back to Chapter 2, where we discussed why some investors actually prefer zeros for their phantom tax liability. What's more, zeros' "false appreciation" gives back a little of what the tax man takes when you keep maturities short.

USING ZEROS TO MEASURE GROWTH OPPORTUNITIES

By knowing that zeros will be worth a stated amount at the end of a given period, you can assess the desirability of a competing growth investment. A zero coupon investment offers a known return over a known period. If another growth investment doesn't offer the likelihood of equal performance during the same period, you know that it doesn't offer the above-market returns that characterize a good capital growth investment, and your attention should be elsewhere. Thus, zeros are one standard for assessing the desirability of a conventional growth investment.

To illustrate, let's say that a real estate investment has the opportunity of producing at maximum a 30 percent total (not annualized) return in five years. However, over the same period perhaps a high-quality zero will produce an equivalent return. What is the real growth opportunity offered by the real estate investment? In this case, not much.

Every investment has an "opportunity cost." In this case, the cost of undertaking another capital growth investment is forfeiting the known return of zeros. The zero will produce a known gain, whereas the *estimated maximum return* on the competing investment is 30 percent in this example. If any investment— real estate, stocks, gold, collectibles—can't produce the same return in a lesser period or a greater return in the same period, you're forfeiting the opportunity offered by the zero. The competing investment's opportunity cost is too high, and you can establish the opportunity cost for a given period by using zeros as your measurement.

USING ZEROS TO BACKSTOP CAPITAL GAINS

Apart from measuring opportunity cost and replacing standard growth investments, zeros can serve the capital gains component in strategies that reduce capital risk. In this case, we use zeros not as a measure nor as a substitute but as a complement to standard growth investments.

Standard growth investments like stocks or real estate don't offer predictable returns over a known period. In exchange for the absence of certainty they offer the positive uncertainty of greater possibilities for long-term accumulations. In other words, you don't know what a common stock Ming vase or parcel of land will be worth five years from now, but it might be worth a great deal more than an investment providing a known return in five years. You trade the possibility of great gains for the assurance of known gains. But by complementing standard growth investments with zero coupon securities, you can maximize the opportunities of both.

By "risk," most investment dictionaries mean variability of return. Individual types of securities offer different types of risks—that is, they subject investors to circumstances generating different kinds of variability in returns. But in a portfolio of many securities, variability can be reduced in the aggregate by altering the mix of investments. In this case, we can couple the predictability of zeros with the maximizing opportunities of standard growth investments so as to remove some of the downward price fluctuations in a total portfolio. That enables high-performance investments to contribute more substantially to your total return.

Finding the proper mix of securities to do this is called establishing an efficient corner portfolio, and explaining it is somewhat beyond our means here. However, most slightly advanced investment texts will discuss the technique more fully. A text of particular usefulness is *Security Analysis and Portfolio Management* by Donald E. Fischer and Ronald J. Jordan (Englewood Cliffs, N.J.: Prentice-Hall, 1975).

For our introductory purposes, let's look at a portfolio of two securities, the first a growth stock and the second a zero coupon bond maturing in five years. Let's say we have about $10,000 to invest, and we'll split the investment evenly between the stock and the bond. We could, of course, alter the proportion to 60/40 or 70/30 or some other fraction favorable to the stock or the bond, and in so doing we would alter the potential variability of the two-security portfolio. But let's keep the example simple.

Our stock is currently selling at $50 per share with a market-estimated average growth rate of 20 percent annually for five years. We can buy 100 shares for $5,000. In this case, the average estimate will place the price for 100 shares at about $12,442 in five years. By average estimate, the market means about 6 chances in 20 of producing the expected gain, with equal likelihoods of progressively greater or lesser gains.

Our bond will be the CATS of 1991, currently selling for about $567. We can buy 10 CATS for $5,670 and secure a 12 percent return. These zeros will be worth $10,000 in five years— a known accumulation. With these figures, we'll offer an amateurish but illustrative example of how mixing these two securities can maximize gain and minimize downward price fluctuations.

Here's the picture at the end of five years under the best, intermediate, and worst cases. In this example, "best case" means the stock does in fact produce its average expected return; it could, obviously, surprise everyone and produce much more than its average expected return.

Possible loss of Principal

	Best Case (Stock = 20% return)	Intermediate Case (Stock = 10% return)	Worst Case (Stock = 0% return)
Stock	$12,442	$ 8,053	$ 0
Zero	10,000	10,000	10,000
Totals	22,442	18,053	10,000

The first thing to notice is that we'll recover nearly all of our principal regardless of how the stock performs. The zeros will mature to $10,000 regardless of the stock's contribution to the capital growth component.

If the stock produces its best anticipated gain in five years, our portfolio has produced $22,442 with no possibility of absolute loss of all principal. That's a 17.5 percent gain annually.

If the stock performs at half its expected rate—10 percent compounded annually—and is worth $8,053 over five years, our total portfolio value is $18,053 at the end of five years. That's about a 12.5 percent return from the two securities calculated on an annual basis. That's more than the percentage return from the zeros alone and more than the percentage return from the diminished performance of the stock.

Even if the stock is worth nothing at the end of five years, we're only out $567, disregarding commissions. If we'd invested fully in the stock and the stock were worth nothing at the end of five years, we'd be out everything.

Because a stock is virtually never worth nothing, we have eliminated the possibility of an absolute loss and assured some gain by backstopping the stock component with a zero coupon component. We increased the total return of the portfolio even though the stock element performed less than expected, and if the stock were to produce more than its best anticipated gain, we'd really be in the gravy—exponential gains with no possibility of total loss, assuming we hold both securities for five years.

If this scenario looks familiar, it should. We noted it in Chapter 6 as one of the advantages of the unit trust that featured zeros as a risk minimizer. We see now that it can also work in the capital growth component of the portfolio through your own structuring of zeros to match standard growth investments.

Note, also, that any of the zero coupon investments we've studied—with the possible exception of EE Savings Bonds—can be used in any of the three contributions that zeros can make to the capital growth component. Consequently, you have a host of alternatives in culling among zeros as companions to the capital growth component.

ZEROS AND BASE BUILDING FOR A PORTFOLIO

Most investors are familiar with the investment pyramid, illustrated here, as a means of structuring a portfolio. The base of the pyramid consists of stable, fundamental investments, usually a home, savings, and other assets that form the foundation of economic and financial activity. The next layer is comprised of slightly less conservative investments, often bonds and blue chip equities. As the pyramid approaches its apex, the investments occupying each layer become progressively more speculative, representing riskier but potentially more lucrative involvements, until the financial pyramid is capped by clearly speculative vehicles.

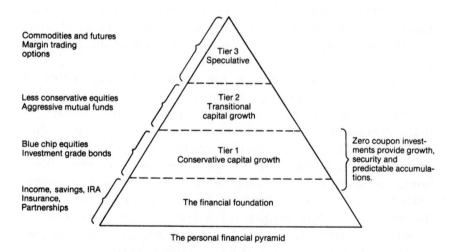

The structure is a pyramid because that figure represents the proportion of a portfolio in its ideal of balance, interlocking support, and risk-return characteristics (low-risk, market-level-return investments at the base; high-risk, potentially high-return investments at the tip). As the illustration shows, capital growth investments comprise the greatest portion of the pyramid's structure, occupying the entire middle. And as the geometry also reveals, a solid financial structure can't achieve the heights offered by growth investments unless it is supported by a strong base.

Creating that base is where zero coupon investments can be of great use in supporting the capital growth component of the portfolio. Thus, many investors won't invest in conventional growth securities without assuring they have a stable financial base that's often constructed with zeros. With their combination of liquidity and predictable returns, zero coupon investments can provide the necessary underpinning for a total portfolio, but especially for the capital growth component. In a word, zeros provide the consistency needed to support less consistent but potentially more lucrative growth investments.

Just how broad the base of zeros should be is something of a judgment call. Some investors use an arbitrary ratio of 3:1. That is, they hold $3,000 par value of zeros for each $1,000 invested in conventional growth securities. If they hold $30,000 par value of zeros, they're willing to devote $10,000 to other capital growth investments. Other investors prefer larger or smaller ratios, but they observe the same principal: They hold their investment in growth vehicles to a proportion of the par value of their zeros.

There's no real criterion for picking the maturities of zeros in the base building portfolio. Some investors use their savings—T-bills and money market funds—as the standard of maturities upon which they erect the growth component. Other investors find that standard too restrictive, so they select zeros of around five years maturity as the determinant of their base. Some investors like to serialize maturities of zeros over several years and use that as the base for determining the capital devoted to growth investments. For instance, they have $20,000 in zeros maturing each year for five years, and they allocate growth capital based upon funds coming due on the five-year horizon.

Whatever their choice of proportion or of maturities, investors striving for capital growth first assure that there is a stable financial underpinning to their growth portfolio, and they create that stability with zero coupon securities. By so doing, they not only erect their investment plan upon a firm base, but they also maximize the use of zeros in other aspects of the capital growth component that we've covered in this chapter.

SUMMARY

Even though zero coupon investments aren't typically associated with the capital growth component of the portfolio, we've seen that they shouldn't be ignored there. Most of the zeros we've discussed can be useful in measuring the opportunity cost of standard growth vehicles, in substituting for those other vehicles, and in backstopping other growth investments. And nearly all can be used to create the stable financial base that supports the investment pyramid. Undoubtedly, smart investment houses—and wise personal investors—will discover other ways in which zeros can be used in maximizing capital growth opportunities. For now, we need to move on to another aspect of the portfolio that zero coupon investments can serve—the aggressive gains component.

The difference between price and amortized phantom interest is capital gain.

10

Zeros and the Aggressive Gains Component of the Portfolio

In the preceding chapter we saw that zeros can be useful in the growth component of the portfolio, but we carefully pointed out that they don't, strictly speaking, produce capital gains. Now that we're looking at a different aspect of the portfolio—aggressive growth—we can recant that statement. When growth in their prices exceeds growth by approaching maturity, zeros do produce capital gains.

To illustrate, let's say that in 1986 you paid $457 for a Bank of America zero maturing in 1992. Ordinarily, this zero would amortize about $90 phantom interest each year, assuming it was issued in a year that requires straight line amortization of phantom interest, as discussed in Chapter 1. Therefore, in 1987 you'd expect this zero to be selling for about $547, as calculated on material covered in Chapter 1. However, when you pick up the financial pages to check your investment, perhaps this zero's current price is $600. The difference between price and amortized phantom interest is $53 (without going through the actual mathematics), and that difference *is* a capital gain.

Whenever a zero's market price exceeds its amortized phantom interest, you have a capital gain. That's true whether the zero is a corporate, derivative, or municipal issue. In a stable economy, zeros' market prices would never exceed their amortized phantom interest, and they would never produce a true capital gain. Fortunately—at least for aggressive zero investors—long-term interest rates are unstable. This market reality makes publicly traded zeros ideal for aggressive gains investors, and that's a separate element of the portfolio we need to cover now.

ZEROS FOR AGGRESSIVE GAINS

Aggressive gains are those that exceed market expectations, and the critical determinant of aggressive gains is volatility—sweeping upward and downward movements in price. As we noted earlier, zeros are extremely sensitive to general interest rates because they pay interest only upon maturity. Without interim coupon payments to smooth out the interest rate trends, price is the sole determinant of yield, and price moves inversely to yield. Consequently, when the general course of interest rates falls, zeros appreciate sharply in price as their yields follow the general course of rates.

In order to have dramatic gains from an investment in zeros, you have to choose zeros that fluctuate in price. That stricture takes EE Savings Bonds, zero CDs, short-term zeros, and near-term zero funds out of the running as aggressive gains investments. In the capital gains chapter we highlighted short-term zeros for their lessened volatility. For aggressive gains, we shun short-term zeros and emphasize long-term zeros, and by "long-term" we usually mean 15 to 20 years or more.

Aggressive investors' interest in the longest-running zeros is somewhat ironic because they don't intend to hold them anywhere near their term of maturity, nor are they interested in yield. The aggressive zero investor is interested solely in price appreciation, and the longer the term of maturity the greater is the volatility that can produce dramatic capital gains.

Although they agree on the necessity of long-term securities, aggressive gains investors are divided about preferring municipal zeros or publicly listed derivative and corporate zeros. Munies present no federal tax liability on phantom interest, although state taxes may apply. Some aggressive investors opt exclusively for municipal zeros to reduce the federal tax burden. Municipal zeros with lengthy maturities also produce rapid capital appreciation, so why add a tax burden if it's not necessary?

On the other hand, some investors point out that municipal zeros are disadvantaged in the aggressive gains component.

Publicly listed corporate and derivative zeros
have ready markets, whereas municipals are
limited

102 / CHAPTER 10

They reason, first, that the "trading lot" for municipal zeros is $100,000 to $250,000 par value, which translates into an up-front investment of several thousand dollars. In contrast, they point out, long-term derivative and corporate zeros can be purchased in sizable par values for a few hundred or thousand dollars, as the trading lot is usually five bonds or $5,000 in par value.

(A trading lot is the minimum par value that's efficiently bought and sold in brokered markets. For conventional municipal securities, about $25,000 par value is the minimum efficient trading lot, but for zeros it's usually higher. With municipal and conventional zeros, par values of less than an efficient trading lot *can* be bought and sold, but it may take a while for a broker to place an "odd lot," and the price you receive when you sell will likely be a bit lower than if you'd sold a trading lot. With publicly traded zeros and zeros in markets maintained by sponsoring brokerages, $1,000 to $5,000 par value is an efficient trading lot.)

Second, they point out that publicly listed corporate and derivative zeros have ready markets, whereas markets for zero municipals are somewhat more limited, even when you're selling a trading lot. A ready market means not only that you can sell easily—absolutely essential for an aggressive strategy—but also that prices are printed in the daily financial pages, making it easier to decide when to sell.

ASPECTS OF AGGRESSIVE TRADING

Whatever your decision about munies versus other zeros, you'll face several inescapable facts in trading zeros for aggressive purposes.

First, what goes up comes down, and the faster up, the faster down. Aggressive gains are possible with long-term zeros, but so are aggressive losses. With slight increases in general interest rates, prices of zeros plummet. (Price moves inversely to interest rates, remember.) Such is always the risk with aggressive investing.

Second, zeros generally produce a phantom interest tax liability while you hold them and when you sell them. In addition to capital gains taxation when you sell (a short-term gain if you sell appreciated zeros within six months of purchase under 1986 law; long-term capital gains otherwise), you'll also have a

As AN average the commission will be 1 90 % face value $1000 / $100,000 FACE + The same for selling.

ZEROS AND THE AGGRESSIVE GAINS COMPONENT OF THE PORTFOLIO / **103**

Trading Zeros.

tax on phantom interest, whether state tax or federal. Even if you owned appreciated zeros more than 181 days when you sold, making you eligible for long-term capital gains taxation, a portion of the gain is presumed to be phantom interest, which is taxable as current income if you sell the bond at a gain.

Third, commissions might be quite high as a percentage of investment and as a percentage of gain. Of course, if you buy and sell zeros through a sponsoring brokerage, you're subject to basis pricing, and that's usually less than an outright commission. But if you're trading zeros through public markets, you'll pay a commission to buy and to sell. As an average, that commission will be 1 percent of face value purchased, although it can be higher. So if you buy $100,000 face value of long-term zeros, you'll pay around $1,000. The same is true of selling. Commissions reduce your tax basis, but they also reduce your gains.

MANAGING ZEROS FOR AGGRESSIVE GAINS

If these considerations don't deter you, you might be interested in some techniques and wisdom from investors who've profited from the price fluctuations of long-term zeros.

First, most aggressive gains zero investors purchase only zeros backed by Treasury bonds—derivatives, in our terms. If they invest in long-term municipal zeros, they buy only the highest-rated issues. The reason is fairly straightforward. Aggressive zero investors are essentially interest rate speculators. Generally presumed to be free from default, government-backed zeros aren't influenced by profitability considerations that are accommodated by prices of corporate zeros. In other words, government-backed zeros are purer interest rate plays because interest rates are virtually the lone determinant of their price movements. Aggressive zero investors figure they'll have a hard enough time anticipating interest rate trends; they don't need the extra uncertainty associated with corporate zeros.

To a large extent, top-rated municipal zeros, especially those insured by backing agencies, are close substitutes for government-backed zeros. The municipal market does not move lockstep in an absolute relationship with general interest rates and prices of government securities, however. They aren't "pure" interest rate plays to the extent that CATS and TIGRs and other feline zeros are.

Second, aggressive zero investors usually aren't diversified.

The cleanest aggressive zero strategy involves two investments: a money market fund and the longest-running, highest-quality zero available. When the investor expects interest rates to decline, he or she moves cash out of the money fund and into the chosen zero. When he or she feels the price run-up is over and interest rates are about to increase, the zeros are sold and the proceeds go back into the money fund, where it waits for the next cycle.

By holding their choice to one series of zeros, aggressive investors minimize commissions and simplify tracking their investment. If they held several series of zeros, they'd have to pay multiple commissions to buy and sell. Consolidating investments in one series of zeros also maximizes returns—if you're right about interest rates—whereas diversifying in several zeros to reduce risk will also reduce aggressive returns. The importance of consolidating an aggressive zero investment is another reason why aggressive investors prefer derivative issues: no need to add default risk to market risk.

Third, aggressive but lesser-capitalized zero coupon investors generally prefer zero funds over direct investment, although the low prices of long-term zeros do make them accessible to the average investor. The current zero funds are invested in felines, which accommodates the default factor, and they offer long-term choices in their portfolios, which is suitable for aggressive intentions. Fees or loads are usually less than commissions—although that may change—and the initial investment is small.

As you'll recall from Chapter 6, zero funds offer a selection of portfolios, long term and short term, within the fund. Generally, investors who strive for aggressive gains through zero funds will rotate their capital between the longest-term portfolio in the fund and the shortest. That is, when they expect interest rates to fall, producing appreciation in the long-term portfolio, they phone the fund and direct their holdings into the long-term end of the fund. When they expect rates to fall, producing greater capital declines in long-term zeros, they phone the fund and switch back to the short end of the maturity spectrum, where volatility is less. Some issuers of zero funds also operate money market funds—the ultimate short-term zero fund. Aggressive investors move from the long-term portfolio to the money fund by telephoning the issuer.

And while we're on the subject of zero funds and aggressive gains, don't forget the zero/commodity funds. These specialized funds don't offer the maneuverability of straight zero funds, nor are they interest rate plays, but the commodity side of the fund can produce exceptional gains while the zero side of the fund is assuring return of principal.

FOLLOWING INTEREST RATES

Obviously, aggressive zero investors are more than casually interested in the course of interest rates. No one is an infallible predictor of that economic variable, and most people aren't good at it when they try to be, but aggressive zero investors try harder than most. There are several indicators that they follow in their attempt to determine the direction of rates, and the first is the maturities of investments in money market funds.

Money funds managers are professionals at following interest rates, and they arrange the investments in their funds to achieve the highest rates. When they expect interest rates to fall, they lengthen the maturities of investments under their control. Consequently, when you see that the average maturities of money market funds are lengthening (maturities are printed in *The Wall Street Journal* and in most financial pages weekly), you know the pros expect rates to fall. That's a clue to invest in long-term zeros, which appreciate with declines in rates.

Interest rate followers attempt to confirm professional managers' judgments by following the yields on conventional Treasury securities, which also are published in *The Wall Street Journal* and in most financial pages. When yields are falling—that is, when prices are increasing—that's confirmation that long-term zeros should be following suit.

In addition, there are other financial indicators of interest rates, and aggressive zero investors also track those. The federal funds rate—the rate that Federal Reserve member banks charge each other for short-term borrowings—indicates where general interest rates are headed. When banks lower the rate, that's considered an indication general rates could fall. The economy doesn't always reply in kind, but when it does, long-term zeros perform well.

Aggressive zero investors also pay attention to the rate of inflation. When it's falling, interest rates generally fall with it and prices of zeros generally increase. A falling rate of inflation is usually a positive for the prices of long-term zeros, but don't forget that throughout 1985 and into 1986 inflation-discounted real interest rates remained very high. Prices of long-term zeros did not begin to move sharply upward (that is, inflation-discounted interest rates did not decline) until mid-1985, even though the inflation rate behaved quite civilly the whole year.

TRADING ZEROS ON MARGIN

Typically, the most aggressive bond investors have traded "on margin." Investors who trade on margin put up a portion of the purchase price for bonds and borrow the rest from their brokerage. If interest rates decline sharply, these investors sell the securities, repay the brokerage (with interest), and pocket their gains.

The Federal Reserve Bank establishes margin rules, and during the 20th century the Fed has permitted investors to put up as little as 10 percent to purchase securities and has also shut down margin trading entirely. As of early 1986, the Federal Reserve had not established definitive rules for trading publicly listed zeros on margin. Inquiries with the Fed and with several major brokerage firms suggested that no one had raised the issue before. Perhaps a definitive ruling will come soon. In the meantime, the following seems to be the operative rules about trading zeros on margin:

- T-bills are marginable.
- CATS traded on public exchanges are marginable, although inquiries with the Federal Reserve and several major national brokerages failed to uncover anyone who had experience with customers purchasing CATS on margin. Other derivatives are maintained in markets by the sponsoring brokerages. They can be purchased on margin if the market-making brokerage will permit it. Again, inquiries uncovered no one who had experience with margined derivatives.
- Zero coupon municipals are marginable as far as the Federal Reserve is concerned, but none of the major brokerage firms contacted had any experience with customers buying municipal zeros on margin.

- The Federal Reserve has issued no opinion on whether zero coupon corporate bonds are marginable. However, the Federal Reserve is willing to issue an opinion if someone asks for one.

SUMMARY

So zero coupon investments do provide capital gains after all, and sometimes they provide them in a very brief time. Long-term, publicly traded zeros can be excellent choices for the aggressive gains component of the portfolio, provided you have the temperament to weather their price fluctuations and the savvy to know when to get in and out of your investment. Whether you choose corporate, municipal, or derivative zeros or zero funds, zeros can serve investors who want aggressive returns. Thus, we see that zeros can be of use in four of the five components of the portfolio, and now it's time to direct our attention to a component of the portfolio for which zeros are the undisputed investment of choice: the lump-sum component.

11

Zeros and the Lump-Sum Component of the Portfolio

Even though, as we've seen, zeros can be used to advantage in each of the portfolio components, they are without question best suited for serving the lump-sum component. The lump-sum component is the least-attended aspect of the portfolio, but it's rapidly gaining the important consideration that it deserves. We'll see why in a moment, but first we need to make a definitional distinction.

In Chapter 8, we discussed how zeros can be structured to provide current income by arranging maturities to coincide with needs for cash. In that chapter, we used the example of an investor who had received a lump-sum distribution from an employer's retirement program. Here, we make a distinction between lump-sum distributions and the lump-sum component.

A *lump-sum distribution* is a financial term referring to a payment of accumulated capital, commonly from an employer's retirement program or an annuity, that is received all at once instead of in an income stream.

The *lump-sum component* of the portfolio is that part of your investment program designed to anticipate your need for a single capital mass for some single purpose. Thus, in this chapter, lump sum refers to an investment plan—a discrete element of a total portfolio—not to a form of payment. Obviously, the lump-sum component of the portfolio pays in a single lump sum. But in this chapter we're talking about structuring a portfolio so that investments make payments in a single capital mass at a future date.

IMPORTANCE OF THE LUMP-SUM COMPONENT

The key to understanding the importance of the lump-sum component is in understanding the circumstances occasioning the need for a single payment of capital. We've already seen two of those circumstances. One was the example of parents anticipating children's college tuition. Parents of a newborn know they'll need a certain sum of money in about 18 years in order to send children to college. Another example was the case of planning for retirement. Most of us know that we'll retire around age 65, and we know how far or near retirement is. Consequently, we know that we'll have a need for capital in a certain number of years.

The Uniform Gifts to Minors Account and the Individual Retirement Account are examples of two types of investment plans based upon the need for lump-sum accumulations, and they're so important that the next two chapters are devoted to them. However, there are other life circumstances that the lump-sum component of the portfolio serves. For instance:

- Some investors will need a known amount of capital to pay off a balloon payment on a mortgage in a known number of years.
- Some investors may hope to open their own business in a certain number of years and may want to begin accumulating capital for self-employment.
- Some investors may be called upon to support an aging parent, occasioning an up-front capital outlay for nursing home fees.
- Divorce decrees are written that might make one parent responsible for children's college tuition at a distant date.
- Finally, there is one reality of corporate life that has made the lump-sum component of the portfolio especially important. Those of us who are employed by major corporations know that continued employment beyond age 55 often becomes uncertain.

This latter is not a pleasant reality, and before you dismiss it ask older colleagues whether they feel vulnerable and dispensable with millions of MBA baby-boomers crowding the corporate ranks. Or ask your more insightful younger colleagues how big they think their piece of the corporate pie will be with millions of people competing for their share when top jobs are handed out.

Beyond age 55, employees present employers with approaching pension liability, tend to occupy higher salary brackets, and generally force employers to confront other age-related conditions like hefty medical expenses. The human facts of demonstrated loyalty to an employer, difficulty in becoming reemployed at middle age, and work experience don't always outweigh the dollars-and-cents reality that older employees cost more than younger employees. Whether it's true in your case, many of us feel that we'll be on our own sometime between age 55 and the time we can begin withdrawing funds from an IRA or other retirement plan. We feel that we have to plan accumulations for those years early in our working careers, and that adds an extra dimension of importance to the lump-sum component of the portfolio.

And right or wrong, many of us feel that social security simply won't be there even if we do reach retirement without interruptions in employment. All of these economic and emotional facts have generated enormous interest in investments that provide predictable accumulations in the future. In accommodating our need for security and financial self-defense, many investors have accented the lump-sum component of their portfolios.

CHARACTERISTICS OF THE LUMP-SUM COMPONENT

The lump-sum component overall is characterized by a known investment horizon and by a need for a known quantity of future funds, and we use the term *known* in an approximate and a precise sense. We may, for example, know that we'll need tuition money in exactly 18 years and, by estimation, know we'll need about $40,000. Or we may know that we'll need about $50,000 in about five years to launch a business. Such knowledge is estimation. On the other hand, we may know that we'll need exactly $15,000 in exactly 15 years to pay a mortgage balloon. Whatever the horizon and whatever the circumstance of the need, the lump-sum component is characterized by a known time period and by need for a known quantity of capital, however loosely we define known. A known investment horizon and a known need for accumulations are what separate the lump-sum component from the capital growth component. The latter is more general with regard to time and accumulations.

With their fixed maturities and predictable accumulations, zeros are ideal investments for the lump-sum component. Whether your investment horizon is weeks or decades, zero coupon vehicles (with one or two exceptions like EE Savings Bonds and variable rates corporates) give you a known par value on a fixed date for a known investment today. When you're looking for dependability in investment planning, zeros provide it, and dependability is what the lump-sum component is all about.

For now, we'll exclude zeros in the retirement-anticipation portfolio because we cover IRAs in the next chapters as a special situation, and we'll concentrate on other aspects of the lump-sum component.

APPROACHES TO THE LUMP-SUM COMPONENT

First, let's take the case of an investor who's working with highly predictable circumstances—for instance, one who needs a known quantity of money in, say, five years. Virtually any zero will accommodate this purpose—a corporate, municipal, or derivative issue, a zero fund with a five-year portfolio, a zero CD—so long as the maturity coincides with the investor's purpose. All this investor needs to do is calculate how much he or she will need and, for all practical purposes, divide by $1,000, the par value of most zeros. Need $10,000, buy 10 zeros—and so on.

Investors who don't know precisely how much they'll need are in a slightly different circumstance, for they don't know how much to invest. Take, for example, investors who are using the lump-sum component as a form of unemployment insurance. They estimate that they need an uncertain sum to underpin their lives, but they don't know exactly how much or exactly when. Investors in this circumstance don't let ambiguity deter their plans. Instead, they generally follow one of two courses.

First, they may prefer to invest short term, buying zeros maturing within five years or selecting near-term portfolios from zero funds. By keeping short, they maintain liquidity and minimize capital fluctuations. In essence, these investors regard zeros as an extension of their savings. Should they be called upon to draw down their holdings, they're in a position to do so.

Second, these investors may estimate their period of vulnerability and set aside zeros that mature during the window of vulnerability. For instance, an investor might assume that parents will need some financial support in, say, 10 years and select zeros maturing during that period. Investors may feel that they're professionally dispensable in 20 years. In this case, they'll select zeros maturing around this distant horizon and hold them for whatever eventuality presents itself.

When investors accommodate the lump-sum component through a distant buy-and-hold strategy, they find that they can receive attractive yields for modest up-front investments. Admittedly, they'll be subject to capital fluctuation, but they're investing for maximum accumulations and are willing to accept volatility in prices. Whether they're direct purchasers of zeros or indirect investors through zero funds, their intention is to invest for ultimate accumulations, and they stick with it.

These investors don't interpret "known investment horizon" too literally. If they figure to need funds in 10 years, that won't dissuade them from buying an attractive issue with a slightly longer or shorter maturity. If they need to reinvest matured zeros or to sell unmatured zeros, they can do so. So if you're concentrating the lump-sum component of the portfolio on the year when you're 55, for instance, you don't have to have every one of your zeros maturing when you're that age. Since you're trying to deal with uncertainty in the first place, don't deny yourself flexibility by becoming imprisoned in a mental and financial gridlock.

We could, of course, continue with other examples, but the idea is established. Investors who expect the need for funds during future times of their lives pay great attention to the lump-sum component of their portfolios, and they often rely upon zeros to provide the accumulations and dependability they're looking for. Let's look at how different types of zeros can be of use.

ZERO COUPON SECURITIES AND THE LUMP-SUM COMPONENT

Obviously, T-bills are of great merit to investors who like to keep their zeros short. And, as we've seen, near-term zeros and short-term zero fund portfolios are acceptable for their market-level returns and minimal capital fluctuation.

Zero coupon CDs present some problems, as do EE Savings Bonds, for some lump-sum strategies. These two zeros are illiquid, unless, as we've seen, you buy them from brokerages that maintain markets or buy large-denomination CDs. Consequently, they're used largely by investors who regard them as an adjunct to other elements of the lump-sum component, where they're exceedingly useful.

Zero funds can be highly useful in the lump-sum component, particularly for investors who don't have a lot of initial capital or who prefer to contribute over time to the lump-sum component. By starting with $1,000 or so and contributing fixed or variable amounts over time, they can build up a sizable lump-sum portfolio element. Thus, they can attack the problem without an initial investment of larger magnitude, and they still maintain liquidity.

Corporate and derivative zeros are ideal for the lump-sum component, although minimizing commissions is a significant consideration. Available in a range of maturities and generally safe against default, they're liquid in public or broker-maintained markets and provide the predictability that the lump-sum component needs. They do, however, usually generate a current federal tax liability when held outside tax-deferred accounts. As we've seen, many investors regard that as an advantage, or at least as the economic price they pay for serving other portfolio intentions.

Given what the lump-sum component is intended to do, however, most investors prefer high-quality zero coupon municipals, even if they're in minimal tax brackets. They reason that their incomes and tax burdens will grow as they age and mature in their careers. Therefore, when investing long term especially, they try to anticipate the need for maximum accumulations from a tax point of view as well as an investment point of view.

(Taxes are one reason, by the way, that some investors elect not to defer taxation of EE Savings Bonds. If you're in the, say, 14 percent tax bracket now and expect to progress to higher brackets, you might be better off paying the IRS as you go rather than wait until EEs mature and pay the tax man when your tax liability is greater.)

Because of their unpredictable maturity values, municipal investment trusts don't generally work optimally in the lump-sum component. They're moderately useful, naturally, for they do provide growth along with income, but they don't provide the known accumulations that are such a comfort in the lump-sum component. Tax-exempt securities trusts present a similar situation. Although they have a sizable advantage as indirect investments in municipal zeros, they, too, have only an approximate maturity. They shouldn't be ignored in the lump-sum component of the portfolio, but they are something of a second choice.

Convertible munies shouldn't be overlooked. They provide the same accumulations as do zero municipals, and with their conversion to coupon-paying bonds just might provide income you need without having to sell the bond.

The great thing about the growing variety of zero coupon investments is that you can apportion the lump-sum component among them. If you can't find a derivative zero maturing when you need it, look into zero funds or another alternative. You can mix and match differing types of zeros, managing taxes and maturities and quality to best advantage. And if the market isn't presenting any truly sterling opportunities during your lump-sum horizon, invest in T-bills, money market funds, or short-term zero fund portfolios until prices and rates and maturities of other zeros attract your attention.

BLENDING THE LUMP-SUM COMPONENT

In addition to mixing and matching for your own portfolio, it may be wise for husbands and wives—or perhaps even business partners—to blend zero coupon investments for total synergy in constructing the lump-sum component. Consideration of tax status, age, life expectations, and career objectives can be accommodated in the lump-sum component among people who are partners in any sense. Many strategies and permutations upon a plan are possible, but here are a few likely scenarios.

Take the case of a husband who is slightly older than his wife. In this case, perhaps the wife might want to be invested in her own zeros and the husband will want to be confined to his zeros rather than to have both spouses own them jointly. If the husband dies before the wife, the usual situation, inheritance considerations might make this an advantaged strategy. As always, consult a reputable tax counsel when apportioning investments.

Also, in this case the husband and wife will want to blend zeros to accommodate their life together if both live. If the wife is investing for a fixed horizon in her life, the husband might want to concentrate his investment horizon with regard to her selection of zero maturities. For instance, if the wife is anticipating the time when she's 50 and the husband is five years older, he knows that the family will have some financial underpinning when he's 55 because his wife's zeros will be maturing. Accordingly, he can examine other maturities and then backfill missing maturities later. His wife can do the same.

Or take the case of business partners. There may, for example, be a time when one partner will want to buy the other's interest in the business. An investment in zeros can help accumulate funds for that purpose. If the partnership is congenial and partners understand the plan, the selling partner can arrange his lump-sum investments knowing that the buying partner is, in effect, contributing to the seller's lump-sum component. The selling partner can then concentrate on other maturities for his own lump-sum component.

Many such permutations are possible. Children can arrange lump-sum investments in consideration of their parents' strategies and selection of maturities. Parents can plan in consideration of their children's portfolios of zeros. To borrow from the sociologist's terminology, you can have a nuclear family of zeros as well as a nuclear family.

The chart on the following page shows how one couple in their mid-30s have arranged a portfolio of zeros by planning for a lump-sum component. Their plan is to have an issue of zeros maturing each year after both are age 42. As you can see, they've been concentrating their zeros in distant maturities, largely because those years offered attractive prices, yields, and accumulations. All zeros held outside the IRA are municipals, and those in their IRAs are derivatives. They intend to fill in the missing maturities as they age and as financial markets provide attractive issues.

By following this strategy, the couple will assure a financial underpinning to each year of their lives together. If hardship demands that they cash their zeros, they'll have an issue maturing each year. Otherwise, they can reinvest the money for continuing accumulations. With about a $35,000 investment, they've already assured themselves of more than $400,000 when their zeros mature, and they've been following this strategy only for three years. If their program proceeds uninterrupted, they'll be very well off in a few years.

Zero Coupon Maturity Dates and Par Values

Year of Maturity	Par Values
1990 (Age 42)	$ 10,000
1991	
1992	
1993	
1994	
1995	10,000
1996	
1997	20,000
1998 (Age 50)	50,000
1999	
2000	
2001	
2002	
2003 (Age 55)	56,000 (Wife's IRA)
2004	
2005	
2006	
2007	34,000 (Wife's IRA)
2008 (Age 60)	
2009	40,000 (Husband's IRA)
2010	25,000
2011	80,000 (Husband's IRA)
2012	25,000
2013 (Age 65)	34,000 (Wife's IRA)
2014	100,000

SUMMARY

For many reasons, the lump-sum component of the portfolio has been receiving greater attention from wise investors and investment managers. There are many occasions in life that call for a sizable outlay of capital, and zero coupon investments can help to anticipate them. By mixing and matching zeros, forward-looking investors can maximize their advantages and opportunities.

With this discussion, we end our examination of how zeros can serve each of the five portfolio elements. The next two chapters deal with selected accounts in service to the lump-sum component—the Uniform Gifts to Minors Account and the Individual Retirement Account.

12

Zeros and Uniform Gifts to Minors Accounts

Thus far, we've talked about zeros in relation to an adult's portfolio, but it could be that your children can benefit from zero coupon investments as much as you can.

A child's largest single expenditure is likely to be college tuition, and most parents have to foot the bill. Unless you plan early and invest with regular discipline as your children grow, their tuition bill will jolt your finances.

Too many parents try to accumulate tuition for children by investing in their personal accounts, intending to liquidate their portfolios when tuition time arrives. That's a mistake because your investment gains are taxed at your tax rate, and taxes reduce the amount accumulated for children. However, if you invest on your children's behalf through a Uniform Gifts to Minors Account (UGMA), you can shift the tax burden onto your children while accumulating funds for their future.

UGMAs can be opened through banks, brokerages, and mutual funds after the child receives a social security number. Parents contribute cash or securities to the UGMA—making a gift to the child—and their contributions are invested in stocks, bonds, mutual funds, and other vehicles that the child legally owns. Because the child owns the investments, gains are taxable at the child's minimal rates.

Each parent can give each child $10,000 per year ($20,000 per couple) without incurring federal gift tax, and the children escape income taxation until their UGMA generates $1,000 in interest, dividends, or capital gains or until the child receives $3,000 in taxable income from all sources, such as part-time employment.

You must appoint a custodian to manage the UGMA until the child attains majority. The custodian should be a relative, financial adviser, or executor of your estate. You can name yourself custodian, but some states would interpret the UGMA as part of your estate and subject to estate taxes if you die. Therefore, it's best to choose a custodian who doesn't contribute to the account.

However, once you contribute to a UGMA your child owns the money or securities. He or she may dispose of the investments at whim, even if that means not spending the funds for the purpose you intended. Also, all dividends, interest, and capital gains from the UGMA must be used for the child's benefit and not for expenses that a parent normally bears. If you use income from the UGMA for your benefit or for customary parental responsibilities, it will be taxable to you.

ZEROS AND THE UGMA

This far into *The Dow Jones-Irwin Guide to Zero Coupon Investments,* we can see why zeros are excellent for a UGMA. Available at low cost in a range of maturities, zeros can fit your budget and your children's life cycle. If you're the parent of a newborn, zeros maturing in 18 to 20 years are inexpensive and just right for the time your child will begin college. If your child is older, there's a zero maturing in lesser time but in enough time for college expenses. Zeros provide predictable accumulations. With each zero maturing to $1,000, you need merely anticipate how many multiples of $1,000 will be necessary for your child's education and acquire that quantity of zeros at one time or over several years. And there are many types of zeros, each with an investment advantage for your budget and your child's future.

In general, there are two strategies for managing zeros in a UGMA: the buy-and-hold strategy and the repeated contributions strategy.

(An attentive account custodian could manage a portfolio of zero coupon bonds for aggressive gains, buying and selling CATS or TIGRs or corporate zeros as they appreciate with interest rate declines. In theory, the aggressive gains strategy would be ideal for minors, who don't suffer from short-term capital gains taxation as seriously as fully taxed adults do. In practice, however, the UGMA would have to be quite sizable for the aggressive gains strategy to pay off, and many custodians lack the skills—just as most parents lack the temperament—needed to manage the UGMA aggressively. Therefore, it's probably just as well to confine our discussion to the buy-and-hold strategy and the repeated contributions strategy.)

As the name implies, the buy-and-hold strategy involves buying a zero coupon security maturing in a desired year and holding it to maturity. Because of the range of maturities available, this strategy works best if you're investing in derivative zeros, original issue corporate zeros, or original issue municipal zeros. You might also be interested in a zero target fund for this strategy, particularly if the fund offers a maturity coincident with when your child starts college.

To illustrate the buy-and-hold strategy, let's say your child will start college in 10 years. You estimate it will cost $40,000 for four years of undergraduate school. As an approximation, let's say that zeros maturing in 10 years sell for $300 per $1,000 par value. You'll need 40 zeros, roughly, to assure tuition 10 years from now, and you can buy those 40 zeros for about $12,000. A one-time outlay of $12,000 provides the tuition. Remember, however, that when selecting long-term zeros for a buy-and-hold strategy most investors prefer government-backed zeros over corporates because of greater safety against default. Still, there's nothing wrong with an investment grade corporate zero in a minor's account.

As an alternative easier on your finances, you can purchase a series of zeros—one series maturing in each of your child's college years. You figure you'll need $10,000 per year for four years. This year you can buy $10,000 worth of zeros for your child's freshman year, 10 years from now, for about $3,000. Next year you buy zeros for your child's sophomore year, and so on until tuition is accommodated. This strategy doesn't take such a big bite from your capital all at once, leaving money for living expenses, other investments, and, of course, your own zeros for your IRA, Keogh, or general portfolio.

The subsequent investments strategy involves buying zeros as your budget permits. Perhaps you can't accommodate even a single year's tuition in one outlay. In this case, you accumulate zeros for your children as you can, buying a few zeros of a desired maturity when current finances permit. If your child is many years from entering college—or many years from attaining any purpose for which you've opened a UGMA—you can afford to contribute modest sums over many years until you're convinced that the UGMA will provide needed funds.

Target funds offer opportunity for a buy-and-hold strategy and a subsequent investments strategy. As we learned in Chapter 6, you can subscribe to a fund with a target portfolio and invest with a single sum or through continuing purchase of additional shares. Target funds are available for UGMAs just as for IRAs and Keoghs.

One problem with a zero target fund for the UGMA is that target portfolios are usually available in increments of five years. If your child enters college in 12 or 16 or some number of years not coincident with the five-year increment, you'll have to redeem shares before the fund matures. However, target funds permit modest initial and subsequent investments, as we noted in Chapter 6, and that's advantageous when you're contributing to a UGMA.

MUNICIPAL ZEROS AND THE UGMA

Financial advisers are divided about municipal securities for a child's portfolio. Munies are of greatest appeal to high bracket investors, and the whole idea behind UGMAs is to take advantage of children's minimal tax bracket. However, there are several considerations that might make zero coupon municipal securities ideal for the UGMA.

First, Congress has repeatedly assaulted tax-deferred or tax-advantaged investments for children. Perhaps you'll open a UGMA for your child and then discover Congress alters the law in a manner that destroys the advantages of doing so. There has been much talk about removing the federal tax exemption on municipal securities, but doing so requires a constitutional amendment, a difficult legislative process that offends vocal constituencies. Therefore, you might want to second-guess Washington by purchasing zero coupon municipals through a UGMA. Their yields are competitive with zeros that pay phantom federally taxable interest, especially over larger maturities.

Second, even if you don't start out buying municipal zeros for your child's UGMA, you may end up buying some when other zeros mature. For example, let's say you open a UGMA and your first investment is a zero coupon certificate of deposit, although our example will apply to any zero that's fully taxable.

An otherwise excellent choice for a UGMA, zero CDs present a limited choice of maturities, usually 5 years and 10 to 12 years, and that may not suit a buy-and-hold strategy. (Special note: as depositaries become more competitive in a financially deregulated environment, they may offer a greater assortment of maturities, so watch financial pages and brokerage reports for changes.)

In addition, zero CDs, like other zeros, suffer taxation on phantom interest. Income from part-time jobs coupled with taxable phantom interest from zero CDs (or any other zero) could engage a tax burden for your child. The burden will probably be minimal, but zero municipals can help you overcome it. By purchasing zero municipals outright or with the proceeds from matured zeros, you can shelter more of the UGMA from taxation.

Knowing you can convert UGMA holdings into zero coupon municipals is especially important if you're doing what many parents do—namely, buy EE Savings Bonds in anticipation of college tuition. As we mentioned in the discussions of savings bonds, these are one kind of zero useful for both minors and adults.

EE SAVINGS BONDS AND THE UGMA

When you were buying EE bonds for yourself back in Chapters 3 and 5, you usually elected to defer taxation until you retired and occupied a lower tax bracket. When buying EE bonds for children, however, you want to declare interest yearly, as the child's minimal tax bracket won't engender a tax liability on declared interest from EEs.

Here's how you can use EE bonds in place of a UGMA—"in place of" because you don't need to open a UGMA in order to buy savings bonds for children.

Through repeated investments or in a single payment, buy EE bonds for the child and register the child as sole owner. Do not list anyone else as co-owner, although you can list yourself, a spouse, or another child as beneficiary.

Each year, file a federal tax return for the child, declaring accrued EE bond interest as income. Actually, you need do this only once for each EE or group of EEs purchased, for that declares your child's intention to be taxed yearly on accreted interest from EEs. Yearly interest is revealed at the rear of Department of the Treasury Circular, Public Debt Series, Number 1-80, available free from a Federal Reserve Bank or branch. Because you're declaring interest at a time when children probably won't suffer tax liabilities, the interest on EE bonds will likely escape taxation. There's no need to file a state tax return, because EE bonds are exempt from state taxation.

However, EE bonds mature in 10 years. If your child is in college then, he or she cashes the bonds and pays tuition. However, if your child is still several years from entering college when the EEs mature, you have to reinvest the cash from matured EE bonds. In some cases, the Treasury may enter the EE bonds into "extended maturity," meaning the bonds will continue to accrue interest even though they've technically matured. The Treasury isn't obligated to extend maturities, though, and even if it does, you might be better off by cashing the bonds and investing in other zeros. You probably won't want to buy more EEs, for your child will probably be in college before another 10 years expire and you'll have to cash the second tier of EE bonds before maturity.

REINVESTING MATURED ZEROS

Reinvesting matured EE bonds presents the same problem as any zero that matures before children are ready for college. If your child is earning enough income from investments or part-time jobs to be taxed, then taxes become a consideration in managing the UGMA. But now we know an option available to you and your children: consider zero coupon municipals for federal tax advantages coupled with the customary advantages of zero coupon investments.

As you'll remember from Chapter 4, interest from zero municipals might be taxable in your state of residence. Some states will tax phantom interest on zero municipals yearly. If that's the case where you live, municipal zeros will serve the UGMA well, because it will be many years before zero municipals generate enough phantom interest to present a state tax liability for your children.

However, as we also noted in Chapter 5, some states tax the total accreted value of zero municipals when they mature. If that's the case in your state, your children could end up with a whopping state tax bill. There are a couple ways around this situation if it applies in your state.

Your state might not tax interest on its own municipal securities. If that's your situation, buy zeros issued by your state for your child's UGMA. You'll escape federal and state tax.

If your state taxes accreted municipal zero interest all at once, concentrate on short-term municipal zeros for your child's UGMA. Short-term zeros won't generate as much taxable interest all at once, so you can manage state tax consequences more effectively.

The current municipal investment trusts and tax-exempt securities trusts are minimally useful for the UGMA, and even then only for very young children, who really don't need their federal tax advantages. The imprecise and usually lengthy maturities of munie trusts make them less desirable than target funds or direct purchase of zeros for accounts like UGMAs. If, however, some day soon an ingenious financial intermediary offers a high-quality portfolio of municipal zeros in a zero target fund, consider it as a potential repository for UGMAs.

SUMMARY

In sum, the investment advantages of zeros coupled with the tax advantages of Uniform Gifts to Minors Accounts can situate your children quite favorably for their adult years. Nearly all of the many types of zeros available will serve the strategy you prefer and can afford in anticipating your children's too-soon approaching adulthood. However, there's another financial passage that you'll confront soon—or sooner than you think—and that's retirement. Fortunately, IRAs and Keogh Accounts can help you prepare for retirement, and zero coupon investments are well-suited for retirement-anticipation portfolios. Our next chapter is devoted to managing zeros in IRAs and Keoghs, so let's see how zeros can help you prepare for retirement.

13

Zeros and
Individual Retirement Accounts

CATS / Discount Brokers

It should be obvious why zero coupon investments have become the most popular for Individual Retirement Accounts and Keogh Plans. Their highly predictable returns enable you to know exactly how much your IRA or Keogh will be worth when your zeros mature, and predictability is a great advantage in retirement planning. Their range of maturities fits your retirement plan whether you're retiring this year or a quarter century from now. Their low prices for distant maturities permit younger, lesser-salaried investors to have long-term growth with modest investments. With zeros' handsome accumulations, you can earn 10 times your investment in 20 to 25 years, and you can triple or quadruple your money in 8 to 12 years.

Zeros also maximize tax-deferral advantages of IRAs and Keoghs. Long-term capital gains from stocks and bonds in an IRA or Keogh will be taxed as current income when you begin receiving payments, so you forfeit favored capital gains taxation. Because zeros would have been taxed at marginal rates, you don't lose favored tax treatment, and you get maximum tax-free compounding.

Zeros are easy to buy. Every major brokerage sells its own zeros, and CATS are traded on public exchanges at reduced commissions from discount brokers. With the astonishing number of zero investments available, you can choose zero CDs, corporate zeros, and zero bond funds if you can't find derivative zeros to meet your needs.

Whatever your preference for types of zeros in your IRA or Keogh, you'll get the most from them if you know how to manage them. There's no formula for making the most of zeros, but you'll want to consider quality and maturity first when you're selecting zeros for IRAs and Keoghs.

MANAGING QUALITY AND MATURITY

Derivatives are obviously the highest quality zeros because of their underpinning by Treasury bonds, and zero funds holding derivative zeros are a close second. Therefore, if you're looking for the highest quality, stick with U.S. government-backed issues.

Zero coupon CDs backed by FDIC or FSLIC insurance are close to derivatives in quality, but there's no substitute for backing by Treasury bonds even though zero CDs are quite secure against default. Corporate zeros can be suitable for IRAs, but when investing long term the quality differential with derivatives is probably worth choosing them over corporates.

In picking zeros of a specific maturity your first option is the buy-and-hold strategy: Select issues maturing during your expected years of retirement and hold them. This is the easiest strategy if you don't want to monitor zeros closely, but it requires you to select the highest-quality zeros.

There are two subsets of the buy-and-hold strategy for zeros in IRAs and Keoghs. First, you can time all your zeros to mature during the year in which you expect to retire. The "cliff strategy," as it's known, has two advantages: You have all your zeros in one place, making it easier to maneuver them if you want to, and when the zeros mature all at the same time, you can reapportion the proceeds as retirement needs and market conditions dictate.

The second subset of the buy-and-hold strategy is called an income stream arrangement. In following an income stream arrangement, you pick zeros maturing during the succeeding years of your retirement. One series of zeros matures when you're 65, another when you're 66, and so on through your estimated life expectancy. The strategy is so named because maturing zeros provide you with a stream of income each year during retirement.

If the income stream strategy looks familiar, it should. In Chapter 8 we discussed how to serialize zeros to produce current income when they mature. The income stream strategy in managing IRAs and Keoghs is the flipside of serializing zeros for current income. In Chapter 8 we took a large sum of money and spread it out among zeros of serialized maturity. Here we take the $2,000 maximum yearly IRA contribution and serialize deposits to produce current income upon retirement.

This strategy, too, has several advantages. For one, it lets you fill in your IRA at advantaged prices and yields. If you stack your IRA with zeros maturing in the same year, prices will go up and yields down as you buy the same series of zeros closer to maturity. That is, if today you buy a series of zeros maturing 20 years from now, the zeros will cost less and yield more than if you bought the same zeros a year from maturity. As you'll no doubt see, the cliff strategy requires you to do that, and it's a disadvantage that the income stream strategy avoids.

Also, the income stream strategy allows you to benefit from new zeros that come on the market. At early 1986, the longest derivative zeros had about 27-year maturities. Someone who is, say, 35 years from retirement could buy the longest zeros and wait for zeros of more distant maturities to be offered. He or she could then add those to the IRA and wait for even more distant maturities to become available.

Finally, the income stream strategy offers the greatest predictability and ease of management. In buying zeros, you know how much they'll be worth when they mature, and you merely cash the proceeds each year of your retirement.

MANAGING ZEROS ACCORDING TO INTEREST RATES

However, the buy-and-hold strategy isn't the only alternative, nor are quality and maturity the only considerations in managing zeros. Some investors prefer to manage their IRAs and Keoghs more actively than the buy-and-hold strategy permits, so they pay greatest attention to another characteristic of zeros— namely, interest rates.

When it comes to managing zeros through interest rates, you have two choices. You can choose the highest rate for the shortest time or the highest rate for the longest time. Let's look at three issues of CATS currently on the market and examine how you might evaluate them in managing your zeros. Prices and interest rates change daily, so regard these quotes as illustrations only.

Maturity	Price	Yield to Maturity	Par Value
May 1989	$630	11.6%	$ 3,000
August 2001	150	12.0	12,000
August 2008	72	11.6	26,000

These zeros are three among the scores of maturities available. We've calculated interest rates from present value tables, and we've assumed an investment of $2,000, meaning you could buy 3, 12, or 26 zeros, respectively, for total accumulations of $3,000, $12,000, or $26,000.

If you want the highest yield for the shortest time, you'll want the 1989 CATS priced at $630 to yield 11.6 percent.

As a yield-conscious investor, you would argue that the shorter maturity presents a high interest rate and greater reinvestment opportunity. Maybe rates will be higher in 1989 when these zeros mature, and maybe you can receive a higher yield in three years. Therefore, you would accept the 11.6 percent offered by the CATS of 1989, hold the issue to maturity, and reexamine investment opportunities when the zeros mature.

This is certainly reasonable, for most investors prefer shorter maturities when rates are undifferentiated, as is the case here, where rates are within 0.4 percent of each other.

However, as a yield-conscious investor, your strategy might also be to lock in the highest rate for the longest period. In this case, you'll choose the CATS of 2001, priced at $150 per $1,000 par for a yield of 12 percent and a total accumulation of $12,000.

There is certainly reason for preferring the 12 percent offered by the CATS of 2001. The course of interest rates is erratic. After all, the CATS of 2008 yield the same as the CATS of 1989. Rates may increase later, but they may also decline. Therefore, why not take the highest rate for the longest time? This, too, is reasonable thinking and an acceptable investment strategy.

ADVANTAGES :- 1) No Reinvestment Risk until maturity
2) Minimises Commissions.

128 / CHAPTER 13

Accordingly, as a yield-conscious investor you can be "right" whether you select an interest rate of 11.6 or 12 percent, for sound reasoning backs your thinking. However, you'll notice that we have a third option—the CATS of 2008.

MANAGING TOTAL ACCUMULATIONS

The yield-conscious investor would think it foolish to prefer the securities maturing in 2008. Their yield of 11.6 percent is the same as the CATS of 1989 and less than the 12 percent on the CATS of 2001. This zero offers neither maximum interest nor opportunity to reinvest advantageously if rates rise. What could be its attraction?

The answer is that some IRA/Keogh investors prefer to invest for maximum total accumulations regardless of yield.

With the CATS of 2008, a $2,000 investment increases more than ten-fold. But there are two additional advantages to this issue of zeros. It is the most predictable among all the zeros, for investors selecting briefer maturities risk receiving lower rates when they roll over matured zeros. In addition, investing long term minimizes commissions.

Minimizing commissions is important because zeros generate no current income to counterbalance commissions. Commissions for zeros detract from capital because they can't be paid from coupon interest. Commissions are also important for another reason: compounding.

With the CATS of 2008 selling at $72, every $72 you pay in commissions today denies you $1,000 in 2008. The more often your CATS mature, the more often you must reinvest; the more often you must reinvest, the more often you must pay commissions; the more commissions you pay, the greater the compounding you lose for not selecting the longer maturity. Consequently, you may end up with more retirement cash even though you receive less in interest by selecting the longest maturity.

Therefore, from the point of view of total accumulations, including foregone commissions, you'll prefer the CATS of 2008. Their price of $72 per $1,000 produces a maturity value of $26,000, which is more than twice to more than eight times the accumulations of competing zeros.

As we've noted many times, you can minimize commissions on zeros by purchasing from the underwriting brokerage when they're initially issued, or by purchasing them from the inventory of the underwriting brokerage after they're initially offered. Brokers charge commissions for buying and selling zeros listed on public exchanges, like those in our example. But when zeros are initially offered to the public, issuing brokers cannot charge commissions. Therefore, you can minimize commissions by buying zeros from sponsoring brokerages. We'll talk more about commissions in a moment.

MANAGING FOR AGGRESSIVE GAINS

If you'll be retiring in a few years, you might not see much attraction in zeros maturing in 20 years or longer. If so, reconsider, because long-term zeros present another strategy for managing your IRA and Keogh: investing for aggressive capital gains.

As we've noted so often, zeros are exceptionally volatile because their return is paid at maturity. Consequently, their prices fluctuate dramatically, and the longer the term to maturity the greater their price fluctuations. To repeat an earlier example, CATS maturing in 2011 have traded between $20 and $175 in the past few years. An aggressive IRA or Keogh investor could have made five times his money—and probably more with frequent buying and selling—even though these zeros are still decades from maturity.

Aggressive management of zeros isn't appropriate for everyone, and given the extraordinary gains possible with limited trading, aggressive trading might prove most rewarding only to your stockbroker. But more confident and sophisticated investors can certainly consider the possibilities of long-term zeros as short-term holdings.

ZERO COUPON FUNDS FOR IRAS AND KEOGHS

Zero bond funds offer an excellent opportunity to manage a portfolio of zeros with discipline, simplicity, and profit. Zero funds investing in derivatives are approved for IRAs and Keoghs, and you can select the portfolio or portfolios within the fund that meet your objectives. Zero funds also permit modest initial and subsequent investments, letting you set aside what you can if you can't make the full $2,000 permitted yearly for your IRA.

Over long periods, dollar cost averaging can work power-

The longer the term to maturity the greater their price fluctuations.

fully for IRA contributions to zero funds. You can have the growth of zeros plus the purchase advantages associated with dollar costing. This in itself may make zero funds your most advantageous choice for an IRA or Keogh.

CORPORATE AND CONVERTIBLE ZEROS

Corporate zeros are acceptable for IRAs and Keoghs, although it's usually wise not to let them constitute a formidable percentage of your holdings. Profitability of the issuer is a major consideration when buying corporate zeros, especially with long-term zeros. Derivatives avoid profitability considerations because they're virtually immune to default, and, as of early 1986, derivatives offered a greater range of maturities than corporate zeros currently offer. These two considerations generally dictate a preference for derivatives over corporates.

However, it may be that a particular investment-grade corporate zero offers a maturity that fits your needs. If so, there's certainly nothing wrong in mixing corporate zeros with your derivatives, CDs, and zero funds as part of your IRA or Keogh.

Convertible corporate zeros also can have a place in your IRA. Their conversion features offer the chance for gains from the underlying common or preferred stock, and as zero coupon bonds they provide the predictable capital accumulations that are favored for IRAs. Given that corporate convertible zeros are so few in number at present, however, you might be better off salting your IRA with conventional coupon-paying convertible corporate debentures if your strategy is to select corporate debentures as equity-equivalent investments. Conventional convertible corporate debentures are greater in number, giving you greater variety and potential for profitability.

ZERO COUPON CERTIFICATES OF DEPOSIT

Zero CDs can be useful for IRAs and Keoghs, but limited maturities generally dictate that they be used to fill in missing or unattractive maturity dates elsewhere in the portfolio of zeros. The chief drawback to having zero CDs be your main IRA investment is what's called an overlapping plate problem.

To illustrate, let's say that this year you buy a zero CD maturing in 10 years. Next year you do the same, and likewise the third year. The problem is that you never have your IRA

Capital Efficiency?

money in a consolidated mass that you can invest for capital efficiency. You've created separate plates of investment, and each plate of capital is at least one year from its nearest neighbor. Here's a visual illustration:

Year 1
_____ (10 years)

Year 2
_____ (10 years)

Year 3
_____ (10 years)

As you can see, you never have more than one matured zero to maneuver if you need to or want to. The step-like gradations of sequential plates of zeros don't permit efficiencies of consolidation, which other strategies and other types of zeros do permit. However, if you're an IRA investor who likes the assurance of FDIC or FSLIC backing, likes to invest in an institution represented by mortar and stone rather than an envelope in the mail, and likes to manage the IRA for convenience, then perhaps the overlapping plate problem won't bother you.

COMMISSIONS AND FEES ✓ *(Maintenance)*

However, one problem that should bother you is the cost of multiple IRA accounts. There are no limits on the number of IRA accounts you can have, so you can easily have zero CDs alongside CATS in a self-directed IRA alongside a zero bond fund. In theory, the greater the number of alternatives for investment, the greater is your access to zeros for your IRA. In practice, many investors have several IRA accounts so that they can, each year, invest where they find the best zeros.

But also in practice, these same investors pay commissions and maintenance fees as the price for accessibility. Fees for maintenance of IRAs and Keoghs are tax deductible, but over a long period they amount to sizable sums. For instance, most financial institutions will charge $10 to open an IRA and around $25 yearly in maintenance fees. If you have three IRA accounts, figure $75 per year in maintenance fees. That's $1,500 over 20 years. If you'd invested that $75 per year in a passbook account paying 5 percent compounded annually, you'd have almost $2,500 at the end of 20 years. If you'd bought a 20-year zero with that $75 per year, you'd have multiple thousands of dollars as the opportunity cost for the $75 you paid in maintenance fees.

Therefore, just as we learned to be wary of commissions as a detraction from capital and yield, so should we be aware of the costs of maintenance fees in multiple IRAs for which we buy zero coupon investments.

MUNICIPAL ZEROS AS AN ADJUNCT TO IRAs

As we've noted, municipal zeros shouldn't be held in an IRA or Keogh because they'll forfeit their federal tax exemption on municipal interest when you begin receiving payments upon retirement. But as we've also noted, municipal zeros can be an excellent supplement to derivative or original issue zeros in retirement-anticipation accounts.

We surveyed the advantages of municipal zeros and convertible municipal zeros in Chapters 4 and 5. We saw in Chapter 4 that on an investment-versus-investment basis municipal zeros outscore zeros in your IRA on several important points, including liquidity, cost, and federally tax-free as opposed to federally tax-deferred returns, although municipal zeros don't provide the tax offsets of IRAs. In Chapter 5 we saw that convertible municipal zeros provide federally untaxed accumulations and federally untaxed current income, neither of which was the case with zeros in the IRA or Keogh.

However, the important point is that you don't have to choose municipal zeros over zeros for the IRA; you can have both, mating tax-deferred growth from zeros in the IRA with federally untaxed growth and income from municipal zeros. All in all, there can hardly be a more advantageous pairing of investments for future accumulations than by combining municipal zeros with zeros in your IRA or Keogh.

There are several ways this can be accomplished, but most investors follow a permutation of the lump-sum component of the portfolio discussed in Chapter 11. In other words, they select municipal zeros maturing during periods of professional vulnerability or municipals maturing to coincide with zeros in the IRA. The combination provides a comfortable financial pillow with ample income—so ample, in fact, that most investors can easily arrange to receive sums in the millions of dollars to support later years if they have the time and discipline and knowledge to take advantage of zero coupon investments.

As we close out our discussion of how zeros can be used in discrete elements of the portfolio and managed for their singular characteristics, we come to the most important point of all: Zero coupon investments of many types can be blended to synergize a portfolio. Although zeros have long been hailed for their advantages in IRAs and Keoghs, zeros held outside these retirement-anticipation accounts can multiply your wealth exponentially. You need not forsake one aspect of your zero coupon investments for another, and by blending zeros of many types you can achieve comprehensiveness and profits in your investment program.

SUMMARY

With the exception of zero coupon municipals and EE Savings Bonds, all the zeros we've met are highly useful for your IRA and Keogh accounts. With their predictability, convenience, and compound growth, zeros can serve your retirement intentions whether you're retiring next year or in the next century. As we've seen, there are several strategies for managing zeros in your tax-deferred accounts, any of which can produce the returns you need for a dignified and deserved retirement.

With proper attention to quality and maturity and commissions, your zeros can serve your retirement portfolio as thoroughly as they serve other aspects of your investment program. And finally, even though zeros are best known for their advantages in IRAs and Keoghs, zero coupon investments held outside retirement-anticipation accounts can provide extraordinary gains for later years. We'll summarize the multiple benefits of zeros by examining some actual portfolios of zero coupon investors in the next chapter.

14

Strategies with Zero Coupon Investments

Thus far we've examined the mechanics of zero coupon investments and how zeros can be used in serving the five elements of the portfolio. We've also seen how zeros can be used to advantage in specialized circumstances, particularly with Uniform Gifts to Minors Accounts and Individual Retirement Accounts. At this point, let's take a look at some actual portfolios of a few real but renamed investors to see how they've chosen to manage their zeros in tandem with each other. In so doing, we can bring home the living advantages of zeros and animate the material we've covered so far.

ZEROS WITH UGMAs

Our first zero investor is Kristen, whose parents have chosen zeros for her Uniform Gifts to Minors Account. Kristen will be 18 in 2004, and her parents estimate she'll need $10,000 per year for four years of college. Kristen's father is a salesman, a frequent traveler whose income fluctuates yearly. He lacks the time for aggressive management of Kristen's UGMA, and Kristen's mother isn't tutored in financial markets. Consequently, should anything happen to Kristen's father, her mother would have some difficulty bringing herself up to speed in the particulars of Kristen's account.

Accordingly, Kristen's father has three goals for his daughter's UGMA. First, he needs to accommodate her anticipated need for college tuition. Second, his fluctuating income necessitates small investments on his daughter's behalf, as the amplitudes of his income mean he must have a steady reserve for living expenses during lean years. Third, he wants simplicity in his daughter's UGMA so that his wife wouldn't be left with a complex problem in financial management should anything happen to him.

To resolve these three needs, Kristen's father has opted for the most straightforward strategy with Kristen's UGMA. Each year, he purchases the CATS of 2004 listed on the New York Bond Exchange. Currently selling at about $170, each CATS will provide $1,000 in college tuition for an investment of about $170 today. He can acquire $40,000 face value for $6,800 today.

Given that his goal is merely to meet Kristen's tuition needs from his irregular current income and not to make her a wealthy young lady, he can pursue several courses in accumulating CATS. In this case, he has decided to buy $10,000 face value for Kristen each year, for an approximate outlay of $1,700 each year for four years. Of course, the price of the CATS will probably increase a bit over the next four years, but probably not enough to deter his strategy nor to erode the stability he's striving for elsewhere in his finances. He reasons that he'll be able to afford an investment of about $1,700 each year over the next four years, and that will be sufficient to achieve his goal of accumulating $40,000 for his daughter's distant education.

Should his financial circumstances worsen, he has plenty of time in which to meet his objective of accumulating tuition money because he started early. For example, if he's not able this year to afford $1,700 for the UGMA, he can contribute, say, $850 to the UGMA and purchase $5,000 par value of CATS, or perhaps only $425 for $2,500 par value. By anticipating Kristen's future financial needs early in her life, he's given himself room to address other circumstances that may arise as a result of an irregular income. His daughter will have money when the time comes, and his family will have income for current expenses.

SAVINGS, LUMP-SUM ACCUMULATIONS, AND IRA

Our second investor is Chris, a 37-year-old public relations executive with a wife and no children. Chris is a conservative investor in a high tax bracket, and his chief financial fear is frequent unemployment from his volatile profession. Three perceived realities guide his financial planning.

First, he knows that his employment is virtually at his employer's will. That means he needs ready liquidity in case he is abruptly unemployed.

Second, he knows that he will probably change jobs frequently throughout his career, with the consequence that he'll probably never be vested in an employer's pension plan. That means he must begin planning early for retirement, making his IRA an especially important part of his financial program.

Third, he knows from the experience of colleagues that continued employment becomes tenuous around age 55 under the best of circumstances. His profession is generally a young person's business, and, lamentable and unfair though this is, it is the reality of his profession, and Chris wants to address it. That means he has a special situation with respect to the lump-sum component of the portfolio, as he must be prepared to be somewhat financially independent in 18 years when he's 55.

Here's how Chris is preparing for his portfolio needs through zero coupon investments.

First, he holds a constant $10,000 in T-bills as a cushion against immediate unemployment. Although his tax situation might better be served by holding his savings in a tax-exempt money market fund, Chris prefers the ultimate security of government paper, and he at least is exempt from state tax on accreted interest from his T-bills.

Second, he invests his maximum IRA contribution in government-backed zeros purchased directly from a sponsoring brokerage. He's staggering maturities on zeros in his IRA so that at least one series will mature each year of his retirement to provide current income. Over the past three years he's selected TIGRs maturing in 2007, 2009, and 2011, when he reaches ages 59, 61, and 63. As he makes IRA contributions during succeeding years, he'll arrange for matured zeros to provide income each year from 2007, when he's 59½ and can make unpenalized withdrawals from his IRA, through 2028, when he's 80. If he remains employed beyond age 59½, he'll reinvest matured zeros for greater accumulations when he does retire.

The glitch in his financial situation, as he sees it, is his relatively brief span of full employment. If his circumstances parallel those of colleagues, his sustained employment will become uncertain after age 55. At age 37, he has 18 years to anticipate curtailment of his career. Accordingly, Chris is buying zero coupon municipals as a form of unemployment insurance.

Again, his strategy is straightforward. He's buying 12 to 20 year zero municipals because they'll mature during his period of perceived professional vulnerability. If he becomes professionally disposable between ages 49 and 57, he'll have income from the matured zeros to support a new career direction or to pay living expenses.

ZERO BOND FUND AND IRA ROLLOVER

Chris's wife Kate is in a somewhat similar situation, but she has an aversion to the price fluctuations that plague her husband's portfolio of long-term zeros. It so happens that Chris and Kate are better off filing separate tax returns. These twin situations compel Kate into a zero bond fund.

She subscribes to the short-term portfolio within a zero fund. This minimizes the market fluctuations she's averse to, and, in her modest tax bracket, the tax on phantom interest is a minimal consideration. As the short-term portfolio matures, she plans to reinvest in the next-maturing portfolio.

Kate takes advantage of the low subsequent investment minimums to dollar cost average her zeros. Her preference for a short-term portfolio somewhat offsets the advantages of dollar costing, for she doesn't receive the full advantages of price fluctuations as she would with a long-term portfolio. Nonetheless, Kate regards her zeros as an extended savings account, and as a saver she's more interested in current market-level interest rates than above-market capital accumulations.

In addition, Kate has invested a lump-sum distribution from a previous employer in government-backed zeros. In this case, an astute broker convinced her to invest for maximum accumulations and to set aside her aversion to capital fluctuations. He argued that the prices and yields prevailing when she rolled her lump-sum distribution over clearly favored long-term bonds, and Kate was reassured by the Treasury derivations of the zeros protecting her against ultimate default. She chose zeros maturing in 2007, when she's 57 years old, and she'll earn almost 10 times her initial investment at maturity.

AGGRESSIVE TRADING

Tom is strictly an aggressive investor. Aggressive stocks, commodities, mutual funds and, of course, zeros are his preferred vehicles. During the past five years Tom has traded the same series of CATS more than a dozen times.

He has an account with a discount broker, and he deals exclusively with the CATS of 2006–11 that we've mentioned several times. Tom is well capitalized. He customarily invests $20,000 when he feels the time is right to move into long-term zeros. That much up-front money gives him control of at least $200,000 par value. Over the past five years, prices on these long-term CATS have fluctuated erratically, and Tom has been in and out of the market successfully. He's presently sitting on a 35 percent gain from his most recent entry in the market.

In his IRA, however, Tom has been invested strictly in money market funds for the past four years. He intends to accumulate $10,000 and then take his aggressive zero strategy into his IRA. He feels that investing less than $10,000 in an aggressive zero strategy wouldn't produce commensurate rewards to offset commissions. When he's accumulated enough capital to provide appropriate returns, he'll invest aggressively in his IRA through zeros.

ZEROS IN EXTENDED SAVINGS

The Johnsons are a couple in their mid-50s. They plan to retire from their hardware store in 5 to 10 years. Building their hardware business has taken the time they might have devoted to learning more about managing their personal finances, but they're still aware of the considerable advantages of zero coupon investments.

The Johnsons invest exclusively in zero coupon CDs with 5-year and 10-year maturities. They like the comfort of having their investment backed by the FDIC, and they've banked for 20 years at their neighborhood depositary. They appreciate the fixed yield on zero CDs because they value known accumulations. They don't plan to withdraw their CDs prematurely, so they aren't worried about interest penalties on premature withdrawals.

The Johnsons could certainly be more innovative with their portfolio of zeros, and they know it. However, they're happy and secure with their zero CDs, and they find mental comfort more important than innovative portfolio management.

ARRANGING ZEROS FOR CURRENT INCOME

Mike, age 65, is about to retire from his corporation, and he will have $250,000 from his employee investment plan in addition to other investments. He wants to invest the $250,000 for continuing income five years from now, as he expects other sources of income to be sufficient for the time being. He expects to live well into his 80s, and he wants to make sure he has income each year.

Mike has decided to place his distribution in an IRA rollover, avoiding taxation on phantom interest, and to invest $12,500 in zeros maturing each year from 1991 through 2006. The problem is that he can't find government-backed zeros for each year that he needs them, so a self-directed account through a discount brokerage won't meet his needs.

Accordingly, Mike has apportioned his investment plan money through three intermediaries. From a discount broker, he opened a rollover that will permit him to buy publicly traded zeros in appropriate maturities. From a full-service broker, he's selected zero coupon CDs and the derivative zeros sponsored by the brokerage to fill in the missing maturities not available through public markets. To round his rollover out, he's subscribed to a zero bond fund.

Mike estimates that he'll more than double his retirement income by apportioning his lump-sum distribution throughout his holdings of zeros.

LUMP-SUM ACCUMULATIONS AND CONVERTIBLE MUNICIPAL ZEROS

Claire is 50, and she has three situations she hopes to accommodate through zeros. First, she wants to schedule retirement income to begin in her early 60s. Second, she plans only semiretirement, having long wanted her own stationery store, and she plans to open her own shop in 10 years. Third, she is expecting to make a large balloon payment on a mortgage at the end of 15 years. With their predictable accumulations, zeros can help Claire attain all three objectives.

First, in place of an annuity she's selected a triple-A rated series of convertible municipal zeros. They'll provide sizable capital growth during their maturities as zeros, and during their income phase they'll provide ample current income.

Second, she's picked a zero coupon municipal bond maturing in 15 years and has earmarked its par value for payment of the mortgage balloon.

Third, having satisfied the two pressing objectives, Claire doesn't have sufficient capital to begin building a fund for her own business. Consequently, she's decided upon a zero bond fund to which she will contribute a regular amount each quarter. Through regular contributions over 10 years she estimates she'll have about half the capital needed to start her own business. She'll rely upon a bank loan for the rest when the time comes.

EE SAVINGS BONDS

Mary is a modestly capitalized investor who has not yet amassed the minimum initial investment needed to enter a zero fund, and she distrusts all public equity and debt markets. Nonetheless, she is a purchaser of zeros through the Payroll Savings Plan at work.

At present, she buys a $50 EE bond twice monthly. She has been participating regularly for several years and is holding about $2,000 par value of EEs.

Mary has no real strategy in her investment program, but she doesn't feel the lack of one as perhaps she should. Cautioned about the illiquidity of EE bonds, she replies that she'll have more than her money to worry about if her EEs default. She is directing her energies toward other areas of her life. Although she could be immensely more practical about her finances, her portfolio of zero coupon EE bonds is safe, secure, and serving her lifestyle.

DISCUSSION

Let's alter the investment pyramid from Chapter 9 so it conforms to the five components of a portfolio that have governed

Part Two. Instead of a pyramid ascending from a base of solidity to an apex of high-risk, potentially high-reward investments, let's create a financial house and put it in order using zero coupon instruments. Essentially, each investor reviewed above is using zeros to serve each of the five components of the portfolio. In other words, all of these investors taken together illustrate how a sound financial structure can be constructed exclusively with zero coupon securities. Here's how the financial house looks when constructed of zero coupon investments.

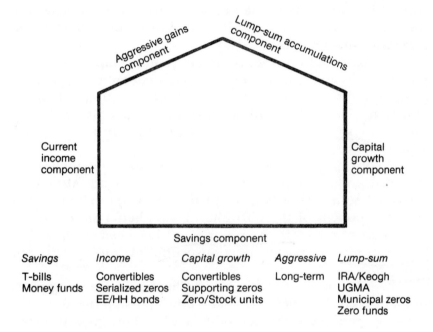

Savings	Income	Capital growth	Aggressive	Lump-sum
T-bills	Convertibles	Convertibles	Long-term	IRA/Keogh
Money funds	Serialized zeros	Supporting zeros		UGMA
	EE/HH bonds	Zero/Stock units		Municipal zeros
				Zero funds

The base of our financial house is comprised of short-term zeros like T-bills and money market funds to create a firm foundation. These short-term zeros provide stability, liquidity, and market-level returns that are necessary for the savings component of the portfolio, discussed in Chapter 7.

The left wall of our financial house represents the current income portion of the portfolio, discussed in Chapter 8. It is erected with convertible municipal zeros, EE Savings Bonds convertible into current income HH bonds, and zeros with serialized maturities to produce spendable cash in hand.

The right wall of our financial house represents the capital growth component of the portfolio discussed in Chapter 9.

Convertible corporate zeros are located along this wall, where they function as a stock-equivalent for capital growth. Although the capital growth component may contain many differing types of securities, it can certainly contain the various zero coupon investments orchestrated in uses for and support of the capital growth element that we covered in Chapter 9.

The left roof of our financial house represents the aggressive gains component of the portfolio, discussed in Chapter 10. It contains long-term zeros purchased for short-term gains and managed with techniques we've noted several times. The zero/commodity funds mentioned in Chapter 6 also fit here, where they can produce the above-average returns that characterize aggressive investments.

The right roof represents the lump-sum component of the portfolio discussed in Chapter 11, and it contains the varieties of zeros and zero funds that meet the needs of lump-sum accumulations. The UGMA and IRA might fit in here also, although they're somewhat separate financial entities from the other aspects of the portfolio.

Of course, few investors would want to build their total financial program out of zero coupon investments. More conventional securities will serve each level of the pyramid and each component of the portfolio in ways better suited to the intentions of each. However, our point has been to show that zeros can serve disparate functions within the total investment program.

The investors we've reviewed in Chapter 14 are using zeros in many ways, but there are many other possibilities for zeros both in strategies with each other and in tandem with other types of investments. Nonetheless, the point is clear: Zero coupon securities come in many types and serve many functions. No longer confined to tax-deferred IRAs and Keoghs, today's zero coupon investments have proliferated throughout the portfolios of knowledgeable and astute investors.

SUMMARY

Each of these investors is using zero coupon investments according to the strategies we've seen. Scores of other examples illustrating how investors are using zeros to round out their portfolios and to complement other investments are possible, and perhaps you've figured out for yourself how they can fit your needs in a variety of situations.

Whether used in conjunction with other investments or in selected strategies maximizing their advantages, zero coupon investments of all types can fill many needs among investment programs for many types of investors. Refinements to existing zero coupon products and new types of zeros are coming to market almost daily. With these innovations will come new uses for zeros and zero-related products. Before we conclude, let's take a look ahead at what new products might be forthcoming and how they can be useful to you.

15

Other Strategies and New Developments

As we've seen, there are many types of zero coupon investments, and many were around for decades before innovative brokerage firms severed the principal and interest certificates from Treasury bonds to create derivative zero coupon bonds. Since then, zero coupon products have sprouted distinctive features, some borrowed from old-fashioned zeros like EE Savings Bonds, others adapted from similar investments like convertible corporate debentures. Investors have flocked to zeros, and financial markets have pursued the strengths of zeros to make them even more popular.

There's no telling where zeros and zero products are headed, but it might be interesting to speculate about their future—not merely for the sake of financial fortune-telling, but so that investors can begin thinking about how they'll use new products to enhance their portfolios.

However, before we gaze into the crystal ball, there's one very important strategy that mates zero coupon securities and real estate partnerships. There are literally millions of investors who can use this pairing of investments to advantage, and either from laziness or ignorance they're forfeiting gains for future years and paying much more in federal tax than they should. Here's one way they can accumulate funds for the future and pay less tax today.

144

ZEROS AND REAL ESTATE PARTNERSHIPS

As an example we'll use a woman of your author's acquaintance whose $45,000 salary places her in the upper tax brackets but who, like many her age, has no tax deductions or write-offs other than the customary personal exclusions and her yearly IRA contribution. Unless a taxpayer has extraordinary medical expenses, there are very few ways to reduce tax liability if he or she isn't a homeowner. As contemporary circumstances have it, millions of young investors—some observers call them Yuppies—earn handsome salaries, but their psychological ensemble rejects homeownership. As a consequence, these people pay out in taxes the money that could be going toward investment. There is, however, a way these people can help themselves, and that's by pairing write-off-heavy real estate partnerships with zero coupon municipal securities to combine tax deductions with federally untaxed interest accumulations.

Having read this far, you certainly can understand why zero coupon municipal bonds are perfect for highly taxed investors. With their attractive interest rates and tax advantages, municipal zeros provide the federally untaxed capital growth these investors need. Considering that most of these investors are—by definition, it seems—below age 40, they have ample time in which to accumulate a sizable fortune with municipal zeros.

The other half of this investment marriage—the real estate limited partnership—is probably familiar to most investors, but it's easily enough summarized for those who aren't.

Like many forms of indirect investment, managers of real estate limited partnerships (called general partners) assemble money from many people (the limited partners) and invest in certain types of real estate activities, ranging from purchase of undeveloped land through purchase of existing commercial, industrial, or residential properties. The advantage for the limited partner is low risk (limited partners generally cannot lose more than they invested), low entry requirements (usually $5,000), and exemption from certain costs borne by the general partner. Just as mutual funds let small investors participate in hundreds of stocks or bonds, real estate limited partnerships permit small investors to receive returns from multimillion dollar real estate investments.

Of the many types of real estate limited partnerships available, the one most interesting to highly taxed investors is the partnership featuring attractive depreciation and write-offs. As you probably know, income-producing real assets, including buildings but excluding land, can be depreciated to reflect wear and deterioration. The real estate partnership incurs depreciation and passes it through to the limited partners according to their prorated investment in the partnership. Consequently, limited partners can claim depreciation and sometimes other expenses related to the partnership on their federal income tax. Depreciation and expenses help offset taxable income, thereby reducing the investor's tax burden.

We can certainly see how the combination of municipal zeros and limited real estate partnerships functions optimally for highly taxed investors. The zeros provide federally untaxed growth, and the partnerships provide federal tax offsets. That combination is preferable to having extraordinary medical expenses, and, according to the way some people like to live, it's preferable to being burdened with a house or condominium.

Before pursuing this combination strategy, though, consider these suggestions.

First, the IRS looks askew at real estate partnerships that offer phenomenal write-offs and at investors who buy into partnerships late in the year and claim write-offs for the whole year. Therefore, it's best to confine yourself to partnerships with modest write-offs, say $1 in write-offs over the life of the partnership for each $1 invested in the partnership. With a real estate partnership, a write-off-to-investment ratio higher than 1.5:1 will probably attract the scrutiny of the IRS. Similarly, restrict your investment to early in the tax year, preferably in January or February. If you invest later in the year, you'll not receive the full benefit of the partnership's write-offs, and you'll excite IRS inquiry.

Second, the partnership has to have what's called economics—that is, it has to have a more-than-reasonable chance to make money as well as to produce write-offs. Lately, a 12 percent return over the life of the partnership has been the operative definition of "reasonable return." If the managers of the partnership don't have a track record in producing an acceptable return, or if they do have a history of being questioned by the IRS, look for another partnership.

Third, select a partnership that has continual offerings and permits investors in one partnership to roll gains and income over into succeeding partnerships. At a write-off-to-income ratio of 1:1, it's going to take a while before your limited partnership makes a significant dent in your tax liability (unless you invest very large sums initially). The opportunity for continuing investment in subsequent partnerships will help you accumulate enough participatory interest to make a difference in your tax liability.

Finally, before joining a real estate partnership, make sure that depreciation and write-offs are among its goals. That may sound like simple and obvious advice, but many partnerships strive for income over depreciation, and such partnerships are for people who need current income. That's not the case in this example.

The combination of municipal zeros and real estate limited partnerships could reduce the tax situations of literally millions of investors. It's something that millions of people—and not all of them Yuppies—could use right now to reduce taxes and improve the future of their finances. But let's move from the here and now to the there and then. Zero coupon investments have undergone several major changes in the brief time they've been popular, and it's certain that more types of zeros and zero products will be forthcoming. Let's take a look at some possibilities.

FUTURES CONTRACTS ON ZERO COUPON BONDS

Futures markets have really blossomed in the past few years, making it possible for investors to seize high returns and to defend other investments by buying and selling futures contracts on underlying commodities. Formerly restricted to farm produce like corn and soybeans, futures and commodity contracts have branched into precious metals, foreign currencies, and, most particularly, financial futures. It's now possible for investors to speculate on the direction of interest rates through T-bill futures, on the direction of the consumer price index with inflation futures, and on the direction of various broad stock market indexes such as the S&P 500, the OTC 250, and the OEX 100.

In order to establish futures contracts, the market needs a standardized or bellwether product to underlie the contract, and zero coupon bonds could easily fit that requirement. If it's possible to have futures contracts on Treasury bill futures, it's certainly possible to establish futures contracts on zero coupon products with longer maturities. Perhaps soon we'll see trading on long-term derivative zeros, with one or another of the issues of CATS or TIGRs as the bellwether product on which the contracts are based.

Zero coupon investors could use these products in a number of ways. For conservative investors, it would be possible to hedge against capital losses by selling contracts for delivery at a specific price, thereby locking in a selling price regardless of what happens to interest rates. Aggressive investors could buy zero coupon futures contracts for their speculative gains or to lock in a purchase price for zeros to be acquired in the future. Futures contracts on zeros could be used in a number of strategies, in companion with zeros already owned or in naked strategies. They could multiply the gains (and risks) of owning zeros, or they could create new defensive strategies to minimize downside risks.

OPTIONS ON ZERO BOND FUTURES

Where there's a futures market, there's likely to sprout an options market on the futures contracts. The trend toward options on futures has been among the fastest growing new areas of financial products, and zero coupon bonds could certainly generate interest in options trading.

Options on futures are an abstraction built upon an abstraction. First, you have a product, like a zero coupon bond, that fluctuates in price. Second, you have a futures contract to purchase or deliver the commodity that fluctuates in price. The value of the futures contract increases and decreases with the fortunes of the underlying product. Third, you have an option based upon the fluctuating value of the futures contract. As the underlying product becomes more or less valuable, so does the contract on which it's based, and so does the option based upon the futures contract.

The chief advantage to the option is that you have a known level of risk. When you trade a futures contract, you could end up losing much more than your original investment. With options trading, you can't lose any more than the premium paid for the option. Options combine limited risk with the potential for high returns, and investors could use them in aggressive and defensive combinations just as they could use futures contracts.

TAX FREE INTEREST ON EE SAVINGS BONDS

A few years ago, the U.S. Treasury Department solicited from the general public recommendations on improving the appeal of EE Savings Bonds. Among the proposals received was one that suggested exempting the first $1,000 of federally taxable EE bond accreted interest. The Treasury did not accept the recommendation, but that may not be the end of the story.

It is clear that the U.S. national debt is a subject of increasing worry in world financial markets. Savings bonds, which pay less interest than other Treasury obligations, could help lower the cost of financing the federal debt if investors could be induced to prefer EE bonds over other Treasury issues. EE bonds already offer many inducements, including ease of purchase and affordability in many denominations, but they compete for capital with other tax-advantaged investments.

For example, the first $200 of dividend income from common and preferred stocks is exempt from federal tax for married couples filing jointly. Municipal bonds pay federally untaxed interest, and more investors are drawn to them as they find themselves in higher tax brackets. Long-term capital gains are taxed at advantaged rates. Why isn't it possible to make EE Savings Bonds more competitive with these favored investments? The Treasury could, for example, make $200 yearly interest from EE bonds exempt from federal taxation, thereby making ownership of EE bonds as attractive as ownership of a few dividend-paying stocks.

The idea is by no means farfetched. We shall have to see if the Treasury agrees. Perhaps a few thousand letters directed to elected representatives and the Secretary of the Treasury could spur the decision along.

INCREASING IRA CONTRIBUTIONS

Individual Retirement Accounts have become exceptionally popular with investors who want to set aside sums for retirement. At present, the law permits wage earners with $2,000 in earned income to contribute that amount to their IRAs, and spouses who don't work outside the home can contribute an additional $250 to spousal IRAs. Congress has received proposals that would permit every American to set aside $2,000 in an IRA regardless of earned income, and this proposal would certainly stimulate sales of zero coupon investments. By stimulating sales and demand for zeros, investors would stimulate financial markets to develop new and innovative zero products.

ZERO COUPON BOND PACKAGES

Among those products might be zero coupon bonds combined with other types of financial offerings. During the past few years, investment houses have issued securities "packages" that combine different types of investments. For instance, it's long been popular to issue corporate debentures or preferred stock with warrants that permit holders to buy shares of the corporation at fixed prices. More recently, financial houses have issued packages that combine stock and bonds. Investors purchase interests that combine equity ownership with creditor investments, becoming both an owner and a creditor of the corporation. In addition, we saw in Chapter 5 that some corporate zeros are convertible into shares of the issuing corporation.

Carrying these developments a step further, perhaps someday we'll see zero coupon bonds as elements of new capital formation. Investment houses could offer packages that have stock combined with zeros, giving investors equity participation in the profits of the enterprise and the assurance of long-term accumulations.

ZEROS WITH PRECIOUS METALS

When silver produced its phenomenal price gains in the late 1970s, some companies issued corporate debentures that gave investors the choice of converting their debentures into a specified number of ounces of silver. This twist on the corporate convertible drew many investors who appreciated the speculative potential of a precious metals investment and the relative assurance of a corporate debenture. Much the same arrangement could be facilitated with zero coupon issues.

ZEROS WITH EMPLOYEE INVESTMENT PLANS

For most Americans, our greatest source of retirement income is the funds we invest with our employee investment plan. We contribute a certain percentage of our salary to the plan, and our employer matches a part of it. Although most employee investment plans center upon purchases of company stock, many plans offer alternate investments, including stock and bond mutual funds, option income funds, and, most particularly, purchase of U.S. government bonds. If it's possible for employee investment plans to make these investment alternatives available, and if the mechanism is already in place to make Treasury bonds available to employees through company-sponsored plans, it is only a short step to adding zero coupon investments to the plan.

By holding zero coupon investments through their company-sponsored or union-sponsored investment plans, employees could add a new source of growth to their retirement-anticipation portfolios. Zeros could provide the predictable accumulations so important in retirement planning and plan management, and over lengthy periods of employment all parties could enjoy the capital accumulations necessary for a profitable and dignified retirement.

ZEROS WITH SELF-DIRECTED ANNUITIES

The tax-deferral features of annuities have come under increasing legislative assault in recent years, and there's some question whether annuities as we know them will survive. The issue of financial survival for insurance-type investment products is an interesting one, for Congress seems to be operating with a few curious inconsistencies.

On the one hand, self-directed Individual Retirement Accounts are congressionally endorsed. You can open a self-directed IRA and trade the funds in your account at will, including purchase and sale of zero coupon investments. But on the other hand, Congress has refused to allow self-directed annuities, insisting that you turn your capital over to an insurance company or financial institution affiliated with an insurance operation for management. Annuities and IRAs have much the same function and consequences, yet investors aren't granted control over an annuity investment, whereas they are permitted to control an IRA, even to the point of making foolish mistakes with money they'll need for retirement.

It would be interesting to speculate on the consequences of permitting investors to have self-directed annuities. For one thing, preserving the tax-deferral features of annuities while permitting investors control over their funds might stifle some of the flight of American capital to offshore banks. For another, it might aid American capital formation by encouraging more people to invest for the future. Many of the laws governing annuities could remain in place, and it would certainly be easy enough to police annuity contributions, including placing limits on the amount of funds deposited yearly, as is the case with IRAs and Keogh Plans, if Congress felt that were warranted.

But most significant for our purposes, having self-directed annuities would permit investors to increase purchases of zero coupon investments. They could purchase them through self-directed annuities much as they do with self-directed IRAs and Keoghs. They could hold their zeros for federally tax-deferred accumulations, garner greater sums for retirement, and in the process just might make us all less dependent on—or less terrified of—social security, with its manifold problems.

FOREIGN ZEROS

Even if American annuities aren't permitted to revise their financial base by offering self-directed accounts, it's possible that foreign annuities might be able to offer self-directed components. Many Americans have opened annuities through foreign sponsors, particularly with the Swiss, whose financial regulations and respected currency have attracted personal as well as investment interest to their products. By default or by intelligent action, foreign financial intermediaries could give their American counterparts a run for their money in more ways than one.

Although there hasn't been large volume sponsorship of zero coupon securities from the international community, that doesn't have to be the case indefinitely. If the American dollar loses some of its robustness in foreign exchange, assets denominated in strong currencies like the Swiss franc or German mark might become more popular for American investors. With zero coupon investments already popular with Americans, it's likely that foreign issuers will tap the enthusiasm.

As the world becomes more international, perhaps someday the Common Market countries will issue consolidated debt denominated in the ECU, or European Currency Unit. It's certainly conceivable that zero coupon securities with international appeal would receive an appreciative audience from private investors and corporate or governmental investors.

SUMMARY

Whether these ideas become viable financial realities or remain mere conjecture, it's clear that we haven't seen the last of innovations in zero coupon products. Whatever financial markets bring in the years ahead, zero coupon products are sure to gain increasing favor from the investing public—and for many good reasons. With their combinations of profitable features, zeros are here to stay, and with new developments they're likely to become even more profitable and versatile.

CONCLUSION

As we close, we return to the premise that's guided our discussion—namely, that zero coupon investments have dozens of uses in a contemporary portfolio. Quite apart from their distinctive service in Uniform Gifts to Minors Accounts and Individual Retirement Accounts, zero coupon investments can provide capital stability, current income, capital growth, aggressive gains, and lump-sum accumulations for today's investors.

The types of zeros we've studied have ranged from the familiar EE Savings Bond to new and untested zeros like convertible corporates. Whether they've existed for decades or won't come of age for decades more, each zero fits singular functions within each element of the portfolio. Together they consolidate into a cohesive whole. Singly or in combination with other zeros or other types of investments, zero coupon securities serve the portfolio with simplicity and predictability.

The strategies we've examined for managing zeros have originated with knowledgeable investors who looked beyond the conventional and saw how zero coupon investments could be used in ways that their advisers and other investors had neglected. Where others saw only limitations, these investors found patterns, and in maneuvering their zeros into new portfolio territory they created new paths for all of us to follow.

We have yet to see the full impact of zero coupon securities in financial markets and American life. With the advent of zero coupon municipal bonds and the spread of IRAs, it is certain that conscientious investors from age 20 to age 40 can retire as millionaires, and zero coupon investors in their 20s can join the millionaire ranks long before they retire. So one consequence of zeros—amplified by an environment of high interest rates and permissive tax legislation—will be a generation of rather wealthy middle-aged people and retirees.

Regardless of your age, zero coupon investments belong in your portfolio. Even if you don't plan to accrue a million dollars, zeros can assist you in achieving whatever financial objective you've set. Whether your conservative intentions keep you invested strictly in T-bills and money market funds or whether your gunslinging aggressiveness takes you into long-term zeros purchased on margin, zero coupon investments can reward your investment inclinations. And even if they don't pay off as you expected, you can always hold them to maturity. No one has to lose money as an investor in zero coupon securities.

With the incredible number of zeros available—to say nothing about new zeros that surely will be developed—every investor can be a winner. Now that you've finished *The Dow Jones-Irwin Guide to Zero Coupon Investments,* all you have to do is put your new knowledge to work in whatever way is most rewarding for you.

PART THREE

Sources, References, Glossary, and Worksheet

Sources and Information for Zero Coupon Investments

One of the most challenging problems that zero coupon investors face is finding a broker who's conversant enough with zero products to give advice. In addition, you need a broker affiliated with an institution that handles a variety of zeros in order to have access to the full range of products. Certainly, there's no reason why you can't go shopping among institutions in your search for zeros—a zero CD from this bank, a zero portfolio from that fund, derivative zeros from this full-service broker, publicly traded zeros from that self-directed brokerage—as long as you remember our discussion of maintenance fees and commissions.

Here is a listing of brokers, brokerages, and other financial institutions with which your author is conversant. The list is followed by recommended reading for further understanding of zero coupon investments and financial markets and personal investing.

BROKERS AND BROKERAGES

Marianne E. Caveney
Merrill Lynch, Pierce, Fenner & Smith, Inc.
2001 Spring Road
Oak Brook, IL 60521
(312) 920-6982

Ms. Caveney is an excellent broker who is aware of the advantages of mixing different types of zeros in a comprehensive portfolio. She is developing a clientele of knowledgeable zero coupon investors and is making something of an investment subspecialty in zeros. You will find her cooperative and helpful and patient with first-time zero buyers.

Mark G. Donohue
Gabriele, Hueglin & Cashman, Inc.
44 Wall Street
New York, NY 10005
(212) 422-1700 in New York
(800) 422-7435 out of state

Mr. Donohue is the best broker of zero coupon municipals with whom your author has ever worked. He also deals in a variety of other municipal bond products as a representative of GH&C, which is a subsidiary of Tucker Anthony and one of the most innovative bond houses on Wall Street.

A word of caution: GH&C is a market maker in municipals. Its inventories move quickly because its clientele is more sophisticated than the norm and because its offerings are top flight. If you deal with GH&C, you have to be prepared to make investment decisions quickly, because GH&C has thousands of clients who readily soak up every new offering.

However, after reading this far you're certainly knowledgeable enough to initiate a relationship with GH&C, and it's the kind of institution that will appreciate your advanced understanding. Being placed on GH&C's mailing list is alone worth a trade, as it sends clients one of the most informative regular market newsletters covering zeros. GH&C is also becoming a larger presence in nonmunicipal zeros, so look to it for selections of derivative zeros and zero funds in the future.

Mark F. Shultz
Shearson Lehman Brothers
Three First National Plaza
Suite 3000
Chicago, IL 60602
(800) 572-9055 or (312) 845-5811 in Illinois
(800) 621-5231 nationally

Mr. Shultz is a very promising young broker whose knowledge of zero coupon investments exceeds his years. He is one of the most thorough brokers your author has encountered, and his doggedness in researching investment recommendations is exemplary. Shearson's inventory of zeros and zero products is among the best in the industry.

Charles A. Schwab & Co.

Schwab is a BankAmerica company and a discount brokerage with excellent order execution and market access. As a discount brokerage, its commissions are less than full-service brokerages, but don't expect recommendations. Your author has five accounts with Schwab, and there's never been a problem with any of them over the years. Schwab has offices nationally. Check your phone book or the financial pages of your newspaper for the address and phone number of your local branch.

Merrill Lynch, Pierce, Fenner & Smith, Inc.
Dean Witter Reynolds
Shearson Lehman Brothers

If you're looking for a full-service brokerage firm to handle your accounts of zeros—and we're talking only about zeros, not other investments—these three institutions offer a wide array of products. However, a good broker is better than any institution you deal with, and finding a good broker is a matter of trial and error. Nonetheless, these three brokerages have issued some excellent zeros and zero products in the past. Try to buy zeros from their inventories, as you'll not pay commissions.

ZERO COUPON PRODUCTS

Throughout this book we've examined several zero coupon products that can be of merit in your portfolio. More products and new issuers of existing products are entering the market all the time. The issuers listed below are the people the competition will have to beat.

Benham Target Maturities Trust
755 Page Mill Road
Palo Alto, CA 94304
(800) 982-6150 in California
(800) 227-8380 from contiguous U.S. states
(800) 848-0002 from Alaska and Hawaii

Benham sponsored the first zero coupon bond fund with target portfolios. It invests only in Treasury derivative zeros and offers several portfolios within the fund. Initial and subsequent investments are very low. Benham is approved for IRA and Keogh Plans.

The Tax Exempt Securities Trust

TEST is a municipal zero coupon bond trust sponsored by four international brokerage institutions: Smith Barney; Kidder, Peabody; Drexel Burnham Lambert; L.F. Rothschild, Unterberg, Towbin. Contact the local office for details about emerging series of the fund. TEST is not a target fund. It doesn't have a portfolio of fixed maturities, but it is very well diversified. Several new series of trusts have already followed the first series, which was issued in 1985.

Butterfield Savings and Loan
200 East Sandpointe Ave.
P.O. Box 25104
Santa Ana, CA 92799-5104
(800) 892-9292

Butterfield offers a range of zero coupon CDs with various maturities and several initial investment minimums. One of the problems we've noted with zero CDs is their limited range of maturities, and Butterfield may help you overcome this dilemma. For further information, ask for Miche'lle Cimino.

Once you receive information, please check the prices and yields on zero CDs carefully. Your author has had several questions about the accuracy of stated yields on many zero CDs.

Paine Webber Pathfinders Trust

Successive series of Pathfinders Trusts are offered by Paine Webber at frequent intervals. Useful in achieving capital growth and conservation of principal, the trusts are available through Paine Webber brokerages nationally. Consult your phone book for the location of the Paine Webber office nearest you, or watch the financial pages for announcements of new series of the trust.

READING MATERIAL

No one text is exhaustive, and new zero coupon products are combining with new portfolio strategies to date even the most comprehensive discussion. Therefore, you have to keep current about not only tried and tested investments and strategies but also new and untested products and strategies. This reading list is useful in helping you make the most of your zeros.

You must absolutely have IRS Publication 1212 and IRS Publication 550. They are free from the Internal Revenue Service.

For an introductory text on the time value of money, buy *Compound Interest and Annuity Tables* by Jack C. Estes (New York: McGraw-Hill, 1976). It's $5.95 in paperback and will help you compute yields on zeros until you're well into retirement.

For an excellent reference about Treasury securities, consult *The Dow Jones-Irwin Guide to Buying and Selling Treasury Securities* by Howard M. Berlin (Homewood, Ill.: Dow Jones-Irwin, 1984).

Call it hubris if you wish, but your author highly recommends his second book, *Life Cycle Investing* (Homewood, Ill.: Dow Jones-Irwin, 1985). It is based upon the Nobel Prize-winning concepts of Franco Modigliani and is a very useful guide to constructing portfolios for differing stages of your life. There is an extended discussion of the lump-sum component of the portfolio, and it is an excellent companion to *The Dow Jones-Irwin Guide to Zero Coupon Investments*.

Among daily, weekly, and monthly publications, *The Wall Street Journal, Barron's,* and *Sylvia Porter's Personal Finance Magazine* are highly valuable reading. The *Journal* is indispensable for buyers of zeros, and its advertisements will keep you abreast of new developments in zero products. *Barron's* is a weekly tabloid with in-depth treatment of financial subjects. *Sylvia Porter's Personal Finance Magazine* is the nation's fastest-growing personal finance publication, and its orientation is toward lay investors who want to know more about managing their finances. It features frequent articles on zero coupon products, many of them by your author.

Glossary of Terms Pertaining to Zero Coupon Investments

Accreted Interest: The difference between par value of a zero coupon security and your purchase price. Also called Original Issue Discount. Yearly Accreted Interest is the amount of accreted interest "earned" each year that you hold a zero coupon investment.

BIGS: Bond Income Growth Securities. A convertible zero coupon municipal bond.

Broker-Maintained Market: A market for buying and selling zero coupon securities maintained by the brokerage that created the security.

Call Date: The date on which and after which a zero coupon investment can be redeemed by its issuer.

Call Features: Many zero coupon investments can be redeemed by their issuers prior to maturity. The bond covenant or prospectus will declare the year in which the bond is callable by the issuer.

Call Protection: The degree of security that an investor has against a zero coupon investment being redeemed by its issuer. Practically, the number of years between today and the call date.

Capital Debenture: When capitalized, a zero coupon security issued by the Federal National Mortgage Association. Uncapitalized, the term capital debenture refers to any debenture, zero coupon or not, contained as part of a corporation's capital debt.

Capital Gain: Sale price of a zero coupon security minus accreted phantom interest.

CATS: Certificates of Accrual on Treasury Securities. A zero coupon derivative issued by Salomon Bros.

CIB: Compound Interest Bonds. Derivative zeros issued by Kidder, Peabody.

CMO: Collateralized Mortgage Obligation. A type of zero coupon security issued by mortgage institutions and broken into a zero coupon component called a Z-piece.

Convertible Zero Coupon Bond: A zero coupon bond that (*a*) converts into a current income obligation at some period before maturity, or (*b*) a corporate zero coupon security that can be exchanged for common or preferred stock of the issuing corporation.

COUGRS: Coupon on Underlying Government Securities. The derivative zeros issued by A. G. Becker Paribas.

Default: An issuer's failure to pay accreted interest when a zero coupon issue matures.

Derivative Zeros: Zero coupon bonds created by stripping coupon and principal payments from a U.S. Treasury Security.

ETR: Easy Treasury Growth Receipts. The zero coupon derivative bond issued by Dean Witter.

FIGS: Future Income Growth Securities. A convertible zero coupon municipal bond.

Form 1099-OID: An IRS form listing taxable interest on zero coupon securities. Required to be mailed to some holders of zeros.

GAINS: Growth and Income Securities. A convertible zero coupon municipal bond.

Intermediate-Term Zeros: Those maturing between 5 and 10 years after original issue.

LIMOS: Limited Interest Municipal Obligations. A convertible zero coupon municipal bond.

LIONS: Lehman Investment Opportunity Notes. The zero coupon derivative securities issued by Lehman Brothers.

Long-Term Zeros: Those maturing in more than 10 years.

LYONS: Liquid Yield Option Notes. A zero coupon bond convertible into shares of the issuing corporation. Created by Merrill Lynch.

Net Asset Value: The price paid to purchase and the price received upon selling shares in a zero coupon bond fund.

Original Issue Zeros: Zero coupon securities originally issued by a corporation, government, or governmental subdivision as zeros. A zero coupon security not created by severing interest and principal payments from a preexisting bond.

PACS: Principal Appreciation Conversion Securities. A type of convertible municipal zero.

Phantom Interest: The yearly accreted interest that a zero coupon security is presumed to pay each year you hold it even though payment of interest isn't made until the zero matures.

Public Market: The listed exchanges through which zero coupon investments can be purchased and sold.

Purchase Price: The amount paid to purchase a zero coupon obligation.

Put Features: Provisions within the covenant of a bond that enable the purchaser to sell the bond back to the issuer after an established date at a specified price, thereby preventing indefinite capital loss to the buyer.

Rating: The alphabetical designation attesting to the investment quality of a zero coupon obligation. AAA-rated, AA-rated, A-rated, and BBB-rated issues are said to be "investment grade."

RATS: Registered Certificates of Accrual on Treasury Securities. Another trade name for derivative zeros backed by U.S. Treasury obligations.

Maturity: The date upon which a zero coupon security produces its full payment of accreted interest.

Short-Term Zeros: Those maturing within five years.

STRIPS: Separate Trading of Registered Interest and Principle of Securities. A special type of derivative zero made possible by the Treasury Department.

Tax Exempt Securities Trust: A vehicle for indirect investment in municipal zeros.

TBR: Treasury Bond Receipts. A derivative zero from E. F. Hutton.

TEDIS: Tax Exempt Discount Income Securities. A convertible zero coupon municipal bond.

TIGR: Treasury Investment Growth Receipt. A zero coupon derivative bond created by Merrill Lynch.

TINTS: Treasury Interest. The derivative zero issued by Shearson Lehman Brothers.

Treasury Bills: Obligations issued by the Department of the Treasury maturing in 13, 26, or 52 weeks.

Yield to Call: The percentage a zero will yield to the date at which it is eligible to be redeemed by its issuer.

Yield to Maturity: The total percentage yield the zero will produce if held for its full term of maturity.

Zero Coupon CD: A certificate of deposit that pays interest only upon maturity.

Zero Fund: A mutual fund or municipal securities trust that contains zero coupon investments. Investors purchase shares in the mutual fund or units in the municipal securities trust as a means of purchasing zero coupon investments indirectly.

Zero coupon securities investment record

Date purchased	Price per $1,000 par	Amount invested	Name of security Number purchased	Maturity	Date sold	Price received	Gain (loss)	Accreted interest

Zero coupon securities investment record

Date purchased	Price per $1,000 par	Amount invested	Name of security Number purchased	Maturity	Date sold	Price received	Gain (loss)	Accreted interest

Zero coupon securities investment record

Date purchased	Price per $1,000 par	Amount invested	Name of security Number purchased	Maturity	Date sold	Price received	Gain (loss)	Accreted interest

Zero coupon securities investment record

Date purchased	Price per $1,000 par	Amount invested	Name of security Number purchased	Maturity	Date sold	Price received	Gain (loss)	Accreted interest

INDEX